“FOR GOD

General John F. Reynolds, USA

To Henry
Best Wishes
Michael A. Riley
Dec. 96

by

Michael A. Riley

Afterword by

Alan T. Nolan

Published 1995
Farnsworth House Military Impressions

401 Baltimore Street
Gettysburg, PA 17325
(717) 334-8838

Cover Photograph, from Reynolds Family Papers (MS6), Archives and Special Collections Department, Franklin and Marshall College, Lancaster, PA

Back cover, from original oil by A. Lamor, Reynolds Family Papers (MS6), Archives and Special Collections Department, Franklin and Marshall College, Lancaster, PA

All photographs cited to their specific repository or donor.

ISBN 0-9643632-3-2

Farnsworth House Civil War Commanders #4

Introduction

In recent years historians have tended to slight the career of General John F. Reynolds and dismiss his sterling contributions to the Army of the Potomac during the early phases of the Gettysburg campaign. Such was not always the case. A generation ago, the foremost historian of the battle, Edwin Coddington, wrote that "if the fates had decreed other than they did, he (Reynolds) might have gone down as one of the greatest generals of the Civil War." Somewhat earlier, former President (and General) Eisenhower had referred to Reynolds as "the best general they (the Federals) had."

Eisenhower and Coddington were merely echoing the sentiments of a number of Reynolds' own contemporaries. On the Union side, his good friend George Meade characterized Reynolds as the "noblest...bravest gentleman in the army. When he fell at Gettysburg the army lost its right arm." Confederate General Daniel Harvey Hill, a gentleman who seldom praised anyone, declared Reynolds to be "one of the noblest of mankind."

My own search for John Reynolds began in 1988, when, as a member of a local reenactment group, I became involved in a movement to rescue the general's boyhood home from the "adult bookstore" that occupied it. To better present John Reynolds to the public, I began to research the man in depth. Beginning with the standard Reynolds biography, Edward Nichols' *Toward Gettysburg*, I then moved into the family papers in an attempt to find the flesh and blood figure beneath the uniform.

Over time my research uncovered a very complex man with a three-sided personality. To staff officers and subordinates in proximity, Reynolds seemed perpetually reticent and aloof, in Meade's phrase: "A man of very few words." On the other hand, to his family and sisters, he was the warm correspondent, the protective brother who would write long affectionate letters pouring out his heart on all manner of subjects and persons. To his command level peers and the men in ranks there was a third, highly charismatic side best captured in a description by colonel Fred Hitchcock: "Reynolds was a superb looking man, dark complexioned, wearing full black whiskers, and sat on his horse like a Centaur, tall, straight and graceful, the ideal soldier." All could feel the force behind those smouldering dark eyes, and in the words of a First Corps aide, "...the love we had for him is beyond expression."

Given the crowded canvas and the full three-day fury of Gettysburg, it is easy to lose sight of John Reynolds, who was killed almost as soon as he arrived. My hope is to acquaint the general public with his early life and give some inkling of his importance to the Army of the Potomac. The fact is, by the late spring of 1863 a great many within the army—George Meade included—looked to John Reynolds for leadership. The measure of their trust in him was best expressed by General John Buford, the cavalry commander who preceded Reynolds to Gettysburg. Under siege from advancing Confederates, the harrassed cavalryman looked round from the cupola of the Lutheran Serminary, spotted the reassuring figure of John Reynolds, and exclaimed: "Now we can hold this place."

★ ★ ★

I would like to express my thanks to all those who made a contribution to this project; in particular, Wayne E. Motts, who recommended that I write the Reynolds booklet for the Farnsworth commander series; also to John S. Peterson for helping me wrestle the ideas and words into better shape. My thanks as well to Tim Smith and the good people at the Adams County Historical Society, and to Scott Hartwig at the Gettysburg National Military Park. Thanks also to Terry Deal for her digital fortitude, and to Michael Kelly for his Pennsylvania Reserve expertise.

Many thanks to Ann Kenne and Janet Dotterer of the Archives & Special Collections Department of Franklin & Marshall College, for making the research a delightful experience. Blake Magner deserves thanks for his map-making talents, as does William Bitzer for his professional reproduction of the photographs in this book, including the original oil on the back cover. Along the way I've appreciated the support of Kalina Anderson, another Reynolds fan, and her packets of much-needed information.

I would also express gratitude to Ann Hoffman Cleaver, descendant of William Reynolds, for her patience with my question filled letters, and for sharing family history. My special thanks to the late Edward Nichols, whose Reynolds biography was of immeasurable assistance; and to Alan T. Nolan for his eloquent afterword.

Last but certainly not least, I would thank my wife Mary, and children, Ethan and Megan, for their support and understanding as I sat trapped to a computer these past months. Having spent eight years listening to me speak of the General, their knowledge of John F. Reynolds probably exceeds my own.

Michael A. Riley
Lancaster, PA

To the American men and women, on both sides,
who served and sacrified,
for what they believed,
this book is respectfully dedicated.

FATEFUL ORDERS

At 4:00 a.m. on the morning of July 1, 1863, Major William Riddle entered the back room of the Moritz Tavern, which was located on the Emmitsburg Road, six miles southeast of Gettysburg, Pennsylvania. The previous afternoon the tavern had become the headquarters of Major General John F. Reynolds, the acting Left Wing commander of the Army of the Potomac. Now, with the approach of dawn, Riddle carried orders from army commander, Major General George Gordon Meade, instructing Reynolds to concentrate his forces in the direction of Gettysburg.

Riddle found the general huddled in a blanket, asleep on the floor. The major felt a reluctance to wake him, which, in the circumstances, was understandable. The army had gotten little sleep in the past few days, and the general almost none. The weeks since Chancellorsville had been a time of wild uncertainty for the army, and for John Reynolds especially. Who knew what dreams might have come to him in this, his last living sleep? Perhaps his mind conjured scenes of the recent interview with Lincoln in which he had been sounded out on the command of the Army of the Potomac, a position he declined. Possibly he saw flashes of family and his boyhood home in Lancaster, Pennsylvania, now threatened by the Confederate invasion. Then again, he might have dreamt of a woman, the secret fianceé whose ring he wore in place of his West Point class ring. Quite likely, in his exhausted state, he dreamt of nothing at all.

Shaken awake, Reynolds lay on his back to stare at the ceiling while the major read the orders. His left wing consisted of the First, Third, and Eleventh Corps. General Meade directed the First Corps to Gettysburg, with the Eleventh to follow in close support, while the Third was to march to Emmitsburg, Maryland. Up ahead in Gettysburg, cavalry commander John Buford had posted his two brigades to the west and north of town in hopes of holding off the Rebels that he believed to be converging there in force. As John Reynolds arose to awaken his staff and put the infantry on the road, little did he know of the desperate race that he and his First Corps were about to run to help save the heights to the south of town. Nor could he have known that his own life would be included in the stakes.

LANCASTER YOUTH

John Fulton Reynolds, born on September 21, 1820, in Lancaster, Pennsylvania, was one of thirteen children born to John and Lydia Reynolds, four of whom died at an early age. His father was a well-known Lancaster businessman and journalist, owning and editing a local Democratic newspaper, the *Lancaster Journal*. In addition, Reynolds, Sr. had served in the state legislature, had been captain of the local militia company, and was a personal friend and business associate of future President James Buchanan—whom the Reynolds children affectionately called "Mr. Buckwheat."

If young John had a predilection for military service, some of it could be traced to his maternal grandfather, Samuel Moore, who had been a captain of the Third Pennsylvania Infantry of the Continental Line, and who had wintered at Valley Forge, as well as being wounded at Brandywine. Besides himself, John had three brothers who served in some capacity during the Civil War, the most noted of whom was his older brother, William, who had been appointed a midshipman in the navy in 1831, and who sailed around the world on the Wilkes Expedition, 1838-1842. This brother went on to serve with the South Atlantic Blockading Squadron during the war and retired as a rear admiral in 1877.

As a boy, young John was educated at a well-known public school run by Mr. John Beck, in Lititz, Pennsylvania, where he was taught such subjects as "Franklin's Theory of Lightning." His letters home revealed an enthusiastic student: "I think I have improved very much since I am here..." He later attended Long Green Academy of Baltimore, and then graduated from the Lancaster County Academy in 1835 at age fifteen.

John Reynolds, Sr. was not wealthy, and by 1836 he had begun looking for a means of furthering young John's education without straining family resources. Not surprisingly, he turned to his friend, James Buchanan, and requested his help in securing for his son a position at the United States Military Academy. John had at first leaned toward the navy, out of deference to his brother, William, but then came to accept the army.

Unfortunately, their first attempt came to naught. At fifteen, John was still a year shy of the regulation age, and a "mortified" Senator Buchanan apologized to the elder Reynolds for the oversight. He promised to obtain the appointment for the following term, and was as good as his word. On March 6, 1837, John Reynolds wrote the following letter of acceptance to Secretary of War, Lewis Cass.

> Yesterday I had the honor to receive from you a notice of my conditional appointment by the President as a Cadet in the service of the United States, requiring immediate information as to my acceptance or non acceptance of the same. I therefore hasten to assure you, that with great pleasure, I thankfully accept the appointment and shall report

> myself to the Superintendent of the Military Academy at West Point within the time specified.

John F. Reynolds was now to enter the United States Army and begin a career that would span twenty-six of the most turbulent years in the U.S. history.

WEST POINT

When Reynolds arrived at the academy in June 1837, he was assigned a tent on the "Plain," where he and his fellow plebes would learn the rudiments of drill. He was known as "Josh" to his classmates, which included such future notables as Nathaniel Lyon, Israel B. Richardson, Horatio Wright, and the Garnett cousins, Robert and Richard. His friend, Henry Kendrick, remembered being "impressed" by Reynolds' "clear and independent thinking, even temperament and courtesy," as were most of his classmates. The next three months would be spent in drill, and though classes had yet to start, Reynolds wrote home in August that he was "very much pleased with my life here and think I shall continue to like it." With the beginning of class, life became hectic, as he explained to a sister who complained of his infrequent letters:

> From 5 o'clock in the morning, or speaking "a la militate" from Reveille, until 10 o'clock at night we have only two hours to ourselves. Besides our military duties such as Guard, Drill, Parade, all the rest of the time we are obliged to be in our rooms studying Calculus, French, Ethics, etc. Cannot even visit our neighbors without getting 5 demerits.

Reynolds was obviously feeling the sting of discipline, and he further noted that Commandant Charles F. Smith was a complete tyrant. Nonetheless, he encountered few serious problems in his first two years at the point, and by April 1839 was looking ahead to his summer furlough and "hoping to get home in time for strawberries..."

In his third year Reynolds wrote that "we have commenced to ride and by the time I graduate I expect to be a great horseman." Later years would prove this to be no hollow boast. His remaining time at the Point was spent learning the duties of commissioned and junior officers, mixed with a bit of socializing. He wrote as follows on January 1, 1841:

> New Years Day was spent, (that is the morning), in conforming to the established custom of the Point, of visiting all your acquaintenances. It is I believe an old German custom, peculiarly northern, and I think a very good one.

In this letter Reynolds asked the advice of his father as to the best branch of service, indicating that he himself was leaning to the artillery or dragoons. At graduation, on July 1, 1841, Cadet John F. Reynolds stood 26th in a class of 52, and was commissioned brevet second lieutenant in Company E, Third United States Artillery Regiment.

SOLDIER'S LIFE

Lieutenant Reynolds' first assignment was the garrison at Fort McHenry, Baltimore, from which he wrote on October 3, 1841, "I have at length made my way to the end of my journey and am now very comfortably situated in our Drawing Room at Ft. McH. in the capacity of Officer of the Day and in command of the fort." He seemed to be pleased with his first assignment, remarking that "the fort is situated on a beautiful spot and must be exceedingly pleasant in summer but a little too cold in winter..." The sleeping arrangements also met with his approval: "Our quarters are excellent. We each have a sleeping room to ourselves and then a parlor and map room in common..."

In November he wrote to his family concerning the possibility of promotion. "I have just seen the death of Capt. Garner of our Regt. in the papers, he died in Florida, which promotes me to a full 2nd. lieutenant..." In the pre-Civil War army promotions up to the rank of major came only within the regiment, so that a young officer could be forgiven if he saw the death of a fellow officer in terms of advancement. The following year, the concluding year of the Second Seminole War, Reynolds was posted to St. Augustine, Florida. From here he wrote that the "officers composing our garrison are Captain J.R. Vinton, Lt. Bragg, Hammond, and myself." Reynolds had always prided himself on his excellent health, but now, in the Florida summer heat, he became seriously ill.

> On the evening of the 12th of July he (Reynolds) was taken with symptoms of fever and since the morning of the 13th has been confined to his bed by a pretty severe attack of bilious fever, and tho' he has at no time been considered dangerous, he has suffered a good deal...I am confident from having been in constant attendance on him that he is

> far better this morning than he has been since the first attack...You may rest assured that every attention has been and will be rendered him by myself and friends.

The above letter and a later one, assuring the Reynolds family "of the continued improvement of my friend Lt. Reynolds," came from none other than Braxton Bragg, a man destined to become one of the more hated figures in the Confederacy. During his convalescence, Reynolds grew bored and referred to St. Augustine as "the dullest of all dull places." But by early March, much to his surprise, the regiment had been ordered to Fort Moultrie in Charleston, South Carolina. Remarking on the turn of events, he wrote that "we know not what changes a week of time make in this unsettled Life of a soldier…"

Life in Charleston was much more to Reynolds' liking, as Charleston society and hospitality made this assignment perhaps the most coveted in the service. As for army companions, Reynolds now found himself in the company of William T. Sherman, George H. Thomas, and Erasmus Keys, who later stated that Reynolds was "as amiable as he is brave." "Cump" Sherman and Reynolds struck up a friendship and attended numerous balls and parties together, including one where their joint diplomacy possibly saved the life of Braxton Bragg. A local swain by the name of Stewart, in proposing a toast to the states of Virginia and South Carolina, referred to North Carolina as merely a strip of land between two great states. Bragg, a native Tar Heel, became enraged and as Sherman recalled the incident: "High words and a challenge passed—pistols for two, coffee for one the next morning, but John F. Reynolds and I from remote and obscure regions like Pennsylvania and Ohio, were chosen peacemakers." Just possibly Reynolds was returning a favor to Bragg for having nursed him back to health in Florida.

In August 1843, Reynolds' mother became ill and eventually died. John was kept informed of her failing health but was unable to attend the funeral inasmuch as "Lt. Bragg is away and I am in command of my company..." Almost two years would pass before he could obtain a furlough. March 1845 found him in Lancaster on a twenty-day leave which was eventually extended to three months. These were eventful times, as trouble was brewing in Mexico. When he made plans to return to his regiment he discovered that they had departed Charleston enroute to New Orleans. Reynolds join them on July 19, 1845, just in time to board ship for Texas.

COLLISION WITH MEXICO

When his regiment arrived in Corpus Christi, Texas, in August 1845, Reynolds was fully behind President Polk's policy towards Mexico and hoped—as a good Democrat—that this President would follow through as energetically as Andrew Jackson might have. The annexation of Texas and the ensuing dispute between Mexico and the United States over the location of the border had brought matters to a boiling point, and General Zachary Taylor worked feverishly to prepare his army as he awaited orders. In the meanwhile, junior officers such as Reynolds went about the task of training the army. His Company E was now converted to light artillery, which required complete conversion to horses. This meant extra work and, for an excellent horseman like Reynolds, extra exasperation: "I have been so much employed for the last two or three weeks, in imparting my knowledge of horsemanship to 20 to 30 stupid Germans, Irishman, etc..." As the year drew to a close, the young lieutenant believed that Mexico was preparing to negotiate and that chances of war were slight.

It was mid-March by the time General Taylor was ready to move south of Corpus Christi, to a location known as Point Isabel. Here Taylor set up a base of supplies, and then marched further south to a point on the Rio Grande, across from the Mexican town of Matamoros. Reynolds received news of his promotion to first lieutenant on the march down. Unfortunately, his promotion involved a transfer to Company G, then stationed in Florida. Rather than leave the scene of war, Reynolds arranged to remain on detached service with Company E during the campaign. In the next month, as tensions escalated, he and his company busied themselves in building a fort.

On April 30, 1846, the commander of the Mexican forces ferried his men across the Rio Grande below Matamoros, with the object of threatening Taylor's base of supplies at Point Isabel. In response, Taylor immediately pulled the majority of his men out of the works, now christened Fort Texas, and moved to head him off. Left behind in the fort was a small force commanded by Major Jacob Brown, which included Reynolds' own battery and the Seventh Infantry, some 500 men in all. Taylor managed to beat the Mexicans to Point Isabel and when the latter caught up, their commander, General Arista, decided to send a column back to lay seige to Fort Texas, an engagement which was to last from May 3–9 and cost fifteen American casualties, including the life of Major Brown.

Meanwhile, fearing for the fort, Taylor decided to march to its relief. He collided with General Arista's force on May 8 and 9 at Palo Alto

John F. Reynolds as a young second lieutenant in the Third United States Artillery. Circa 1845–1846. *(Courtesy Franklin and Marshall College)*

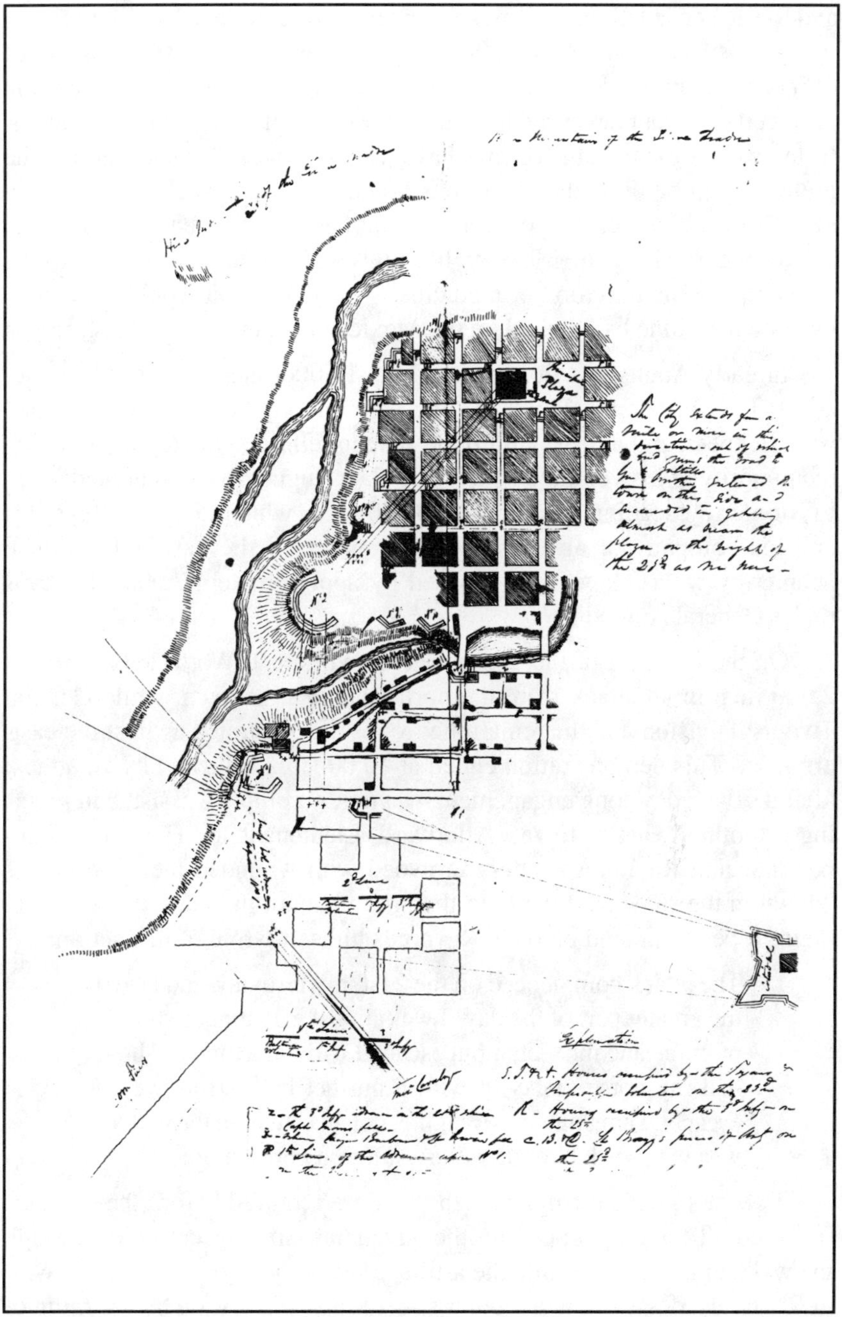

Battle of Monterrey, September 21, 1846. From a map drawn by First Lieutenant John F. Reynolds, from the Franklin and Marshall Archives.

and Resaca de la Palma, where the Mexicans were trounced and sent flying back across the river. Back at Fort Texas—renamed Fort Brown in honor of its dead commander—Reynolds wrote home as follows: "Of one thing I am certain, I can never again, I don't think, be placed in a more uncomfortable situation than the one we have just got out of..." He added that he preferred ten battlefields to a weeks bombardment "...such as we had in Fort Brown..." Later the young lieutenant had the chance to see the other side of war; visiting the Mexican hospitals and handing out money to the soldiers, who had no food or medicine. "How different would have been our fate if fortune had picked on the Mexican banner in these battles."

In early August, Taylor marched his 15,000-man force to Camargo, across the river on the Mexican side. Very quickly his army was plagued with sickness, and at least a third of the men fell ill, many to die. Leaving the majority of his volunteers behind, in late August Taylor marched south to Monterrey, leading a column of 6,000 men, which included Reynolds and his company of artillery. On September 19 they arrived opposite Monterrey where they were opposed by approximately 7,000 Mexicans under General Ampudia.

On the morning of the 21st, General William J. Worth led a force of 2,000 men in an attack from the north and west of town, while General Twiggs' Division and the remaining troops demonstrated against the eastern side. This demonstration ended at 10:00 a.m., followed by an attack; after a severe day-long engagement, Reynolds' company assisted in securing a foothold east of town. Afterward, Lieutenant Joe Hooker remembered seeing Reynolds' battery crowded with wounded men and horses "down in the same spot, making the ground about the guns slippery with their gasped foam and blood." Reynolds himself wrote of this action:

> The attack commenced on the 21st, my birthday, and lasted the greater part of the day. I was amidst a continuos shower of grape and musqetry, but escaped without a touch. Tho' I had my horse twice hit with a musqet ball. How we all escaped I am unable to imagine, not an officer in the battery was wounded, but our battery suffered considerable.

Two more days of rugged fighting were required before the city surrendered. To avoid sniper fire, the advancing infantry cut holes through the walls of the house, while the artillery swept the narrow streets. It was, in Reynolds' description, a regular street fight. Finally, on the morning of the 25th, Ampudia surrendered, and, after difficult negotiations, his men were allowed to march out with their sidearms, flags, and personal property. Watching the Mexicans depart, Reynolds noted that "...about 7,000 troops left for Sallito, as mean a looking rabble as a man ever set eyes upon..."

"WE ARE PRETTY WELL USED UP"

In mid-December Taylor marched his 2,000-man column south to Victoria. During this trek Reynolds and another company officer, Sam French, decided to celebrate New Year's Day, 1847, with a batch of egg-nog. Having procured some eggs, they unfortunately came up short on liquor. This conundrum they solved by calling the company doctor to their quarters and placing him under arrest until he agreed to provide bottles of rum and brandy from company medical supplies. As a reward, he was allowed to share in the eggnog.

Two weeks later, Taylor's column would be back where it started, with little to show for the effort. Arriving in his old camp, Taylor discovered that General Winfield Scott had been there and gone—taking with him the bulk of Taylor's reserve infantry. Recently breveted to lieutenant general and given command of the Mexico City expedition, Scott exercised his prerogative to commandeer a portion of Taylor's battle-tested "regulars." In a letter home, Reynolds vented the feelings of those left behind: "General Taylor is perfectly disgusted with the part assigned to him here...He certainly never expected the treatment he has now received at their hands, withdrawing all the regular troops and part of the volunteers..." Meanwhile, Taylor had evidently become impressed with Reynolds. During this period one of the general's aides, William Bliss, wrote a West Point acquaintance that "your young friend [Reynolds] has the general's high regard, and is the idol of his men."

By now, Santa Anna had assumed personal command of the Mexican army. In desperate need of a victory, he decided to march his 20,000-man force north to attack Taylor's 4,500 Americans at their camp near Aqua Nueva. Fully aware of the latter's intentions, Taylor pulled his own force north to a better defensive position on the heights of a valley overlooking the Buena Vista hacienda.

On February 22, 1847, Santa Anna attacked the American outposts and then offered Taylor a chance to surrender. In remembrance of George Washington's birthday, Taylor spurned the offer and the Mexicans attacked at 3:00 p.m., fighting till dark, with minimal gain. The following morning Reynolds was able to grab a quick breakfast of ham and hard bread, and, before taking his post, wrote that "I never went into action in better spirits in my life..."

The Mexicans resumed their attacks on the left and center of the American line, and Reynolds' company, now commanded by Captain Thomas Sherman, was brought to the front. Somewhat later, however, Reynolds' two-gun section was ordered to help repel a Mexican breakthrough near the hacienda. Here, in the words of one soldier, Reynolds' section fired "with astonishing accuracy and execution." Shortly after, when the American left flank was hit, Reynolds was pulled back to help Colonel Jefferson Davis and his regiment of Mississippi Rifles. Santa Anna made one more attempt to break the American lines, sending a 12,000-man assault against the American center, but this final attack sputtered in the face of stiff resistance, which included Reynolds' guns, and the Mexicans were forced to abandon the field.

Later that day Abner Doubleday found Reynolds leaning on a cannon near the spot of the attack, and asked him his thoughts when all of those Mexican soldiers began coming his way. Reynolds replied that he did "not allow myself to think on that subject, for I might have thought wrong." He later wrote that "this has been the greatest battle yet, I thought that at Monterrey I had been in a pretty tight place but it was nothing to this...We are pretty well used up, both men and horses..."

Little did Reynolds know that his own war was now over, even though he would spend another twenty months in Mexico. Taylor's army would now sit on the sidelines and watch as Scott moved to take Mexico City. During this stretch Reynolds grew quite weary of his surroundings and asked his father to try to use his influence to get him ordered to West Point as an instructor. "I am almost sick of the people of this country and everything in it..."

The twenty-seven-year-old bachelor also seemed to be experiencing pangs of another sort. Writing on New Year's Day, 1848, Reynolds informed his sister, Jane, that he was granting her full power to receive proposals from any of the female population at home. He had but three requirements: "the applicant must be good looking, amiable, and have a small portion of what is usually termed common sense," not that he would object to her having a bit of money. He ended by saying "enough of nonsense," but one can sense that the loneliness of army life was beginning to wear on John Reynolds.

Though Reynolds, Sr. was unable to obtain an appointment to West Point, he did write to his old friend, James Buchanan, now Secretary of

State, asking him to look after John, referring obviously to brevets (commissions of honorary rank). Buchanan was more than willing to assist, replying that "I shall take good care of John when the proper time arrives. He richly deserves a brevet..." Reynolds professed himself indifferent, writing that: "All I care for and all the reward I expect is the good opinion of my brother officers in the Army and my friends at home..." Of course Reynolds coveted them as much as any young officer in the regular army, but until he was awarded one, he remained a bit skeptical of their worth. Soon thereafter he received two brevets, one as captain and one as major for services at Monterrey and Buena Vista. In career terms, his Mexican adventure had been a success.

1850s SERVICE

December 1848 found John Reynolds back in Lancaster on his first leave in over three years. The veteran of Mexico had changed dramatically since his last visit. The long locks of shoulder length hair were gone, cut off during the siege of Fort Brown when the heat had become unbearable. The slender six-footer was sporting a new mustache and beard, of which he was quite proud, and discerning family members could also detect a change within. In his time away, in the process of leading troops under fire, he had greatly matured.

The citizens of Lancaster were quite pleased to learn that the local "hero" of Buena Vista was amongst them, and decided to offer him a social dinner, "...as a small token of their regard and admiration for your brave and meritorious conduct in the several battles, in which you were engaged..." But, Reynolds surprisingly declined the honor, and in so doing undoubtedly passed on the chance to meet a number of eligible young ladies.

> Your letter of to-day, offering me a "social dinner" was received with deep emotions, and I regret that my short stay among my fellow citizens of Lancaster compels me to decline the honor. Allow me to assure you that no feelings are more gratifying to the soldier than those excited by the approbation of his fellow country-men; and that this testimony of your approval of my conduct in the service of my country will ever be most gratefully cherished by me.

In January 1849, Reynolds reported to Company G at Fort Preble, Maine, which was to be his home for the next four years. Once again he encountered garrison life with its interminable paperwork: "...it is 1 o'clock and I have a pile of papers as high as my head on my table..." A more critical complaint was the lack of good cigars, the local ones being but "trash," and he begged his sisters at home to send him the mildest smokes from Lancaster. To help him stave off the winter cold, his sister Harriet knitted a scarf that became the envy of the entire post, including his dog Milo, who "...seized it in his mouth and paws..." and might have reduced it to its original condition had Reynolds not come to its rescue.

January 1853 found him transferred to General Twiggs' staff in New Orleans. An epidemic of yellow fever ravaged the city that year, and as the officers and men fled the city, Reynolds volunteered to stay, taking the place of his friend "Cump" Sherman, who with his family, was awaiting furlough. To Reynolds' shock and dismay, he himself came down with the fever, but was able to quickly recover.

By summer, he was again on leave when his father tragically succumbed to a massive stroke while visiting his daughter Jane in Baltimore. By the end of the year orders caught up with him, and in January 1854, Reynolds had comfortably settled in at Fort Lafayette, New York. During this winter the loneliness of garrison life seemed especially to lay heavy. "...I have been solitary and alone for one week, without seeing a soul that I could talk to..."

The following spring, the two companies of the Third Artillery, of which Reynolds had temporary command, were ordered to prepare for an overland march to California. Their first stop was Fort Leavenworth, Kansas, where the expedition commander, Brevet Lt. Col. Edward Steptoe, was assembling his force. Their march commenced in early June and the column arrived at Salt Lake City on August 3. Here Reynolds had his first introduction to Brigham Young's Mormons—"made the acquaintance of several families, yet this did not give us entree to their houses"—and was highly irritated by their clannishness. His feelings toward them hardened after he had brought in a group of Indians charged with massacring a band of army engineers, only to see a Mormon court let them off with manslaughter..."I cannot write the truth about these people here, but will sometime or other..." In May 1855, he was off on the final leg of his journey to California, reaching Benicia Barracks in late July. He was also sporting a new rank, as word had come in March of his promotion to the regular rank of captain.

But, there was another promotion that he wanted just as much. Reynolds' old friend, Braxton Bragg, had been commissioned as a major in the cavalry arm, which meant that Bragg would be giving up his light artillery company, a unit that Reynolds wanted badly to command. Pulling out the stops, he wrote to his brother James, a lawyer with political clout and the ear of James Buchanan, soon to be elected President: "...I wish you would use any and all the political influence you may have to get me that Co..." Upon reaching California, he learned that Bragg had declined the cavalry commission, though there were rumors that he might resign from the army. Later came news that Bragg would indeed resign the following February, but that General Scott had recommended Robert Anderson for Bragg's position. In a letter to brother James that August, Reynolds' spirits were clearly sagging. "Merit is no recommendation and political influence everything...I may say that I have never been so disgusted with this army as within the last twelve months." In recent years he had watched a number of northern-born officers resign to pursue more lucrative civilian careers. He might threaten to do so himself, but never did, though his letters would reflect a sense of frustration for months to come.

Reynolds was then ordered to Fort Orford, Oregon to assume command of Company H, Third Artillery. His trip north aboard the steamer *California* became one of the more perilous episodes of his life. As the ship entered the mouth of the Columbia River, a boiler burst, setting it on fire to drift toward the bar. The officers and soldiers assisted the crew in gaining control, but the ship was forced to return to San Francisco for repairs, and Reynolds was unable to report to his new post until January 1856.

In March the Captain was caught up in his first Indian war, a campaign that required Reynolds' artillery and a regiment of infantry to chase a band of Rogue River Indians through some extremely rugged and mountainous country:

> It is now three months since I left Ft. Orford, with my co., to take the field against the indians who had committed the outrages on the settlers at this place...and after a very laborious and fatiguing campaign with occasional skirmishing through the mountains, we have succeeded them all, or nearly all, to come in, give up their arms.

He further noted that a band of hostiles still remained up in the mountains, and that he and Captain Edward Ord would have to go after them to bring them in. The two officers and their men must have done a credible job, for thirteen of the leading citizens of Fort Orford later joined in presenting Reynolds a gold watch.

> Representing a portion of our fellow citizens who, desirous of manifesting the high esteem in which you are held by them, as an Officer, and for the interest shown by you

> for us, during our defenseless condition while you were in command of the Military Post, at this place. We ask your acceptance of the accompanying Gold Watch, as a small token of our high consideration and regard.

Orders now reached Reynolds giving him the light artillery company he had coveted for the past year, but it was a hollow victory. The War Department had decided to replace the light artillery with long-range guns, thereby destroying the "finest battery" that Braxton Bragg had even seen. Reynolds now commanded Company C, and was ordered to Fort Monroe, Virginia, where he arrived by the end of the year. This transfer to the East enabled him to take part in the accounting of his father's estate, a job that, in Reynolds' opinion, had been badly botched by his brother James. Reynolds' primary family concern was his two unmarried sisters, Harriet and Eleanor. He had always been the protective big brother to them, and he assured them that any deficiency caused by James' mishandling of the estate would be made up by himself. Lacking a family of his own while living the gypsy life of a soldier, Reynolds channeled his affection toward his siblings.

His impatience to clear up the estate was rooted in the knowledge that he would be off to Utah in the spring. Trouble was brewing with the Mormons; stories of three federal judges claiming to have been run out of the territory prompted President Buchanan to appoint a new governor, and in May 1857, Colonel Albert Sidney Johnston had been ordered to lead an expedition to Salt Lake City to reassert Federal authority. The Mormons mobilized their forces and harassed Johnston's column by stealing oxen, burning grazing lands, and destroying wagons. Short on supplies, Johnston and his force of 2,000 spent a bitter winter at Fort Bridger, Utah.

By the time Reynolds arrived at Camp Floyd, Utah Territory, in September 1858, President Buchanan's envoy had negotiated a settlement. The Federally appointed governor claimed his office, the grievances of the church were addressed, and the "Mormon War" was over. Nonetheless, Reynolds' old bitterness spilled in a letter home. The war in Utah had ended, "but I put no faith in anything of the kind, and will not believe it until the Mormons are out of our territory..."

He spent the next twelve months at Camp Floyd near Salt Lake City before being ordered to Oregon, in early September 1859. Though far to the west, Reynolds kept abreast of mounting tensions in the East and was clearly appalled by John Brown's raid on Harpers Ferry. Politically speaking, Reynolds was an old-line Democrat whose family had close ties with the Buchanan administration. Like most northern-born West Pointers,

Reynolds was a social conservative for whom slavery was not an issue. In his opinion: "If they could hang, along with old Brown...a few more of the abolitionist stripe, it would effectively stop this agitation for a time..."

On the other hand, Reynolds was a strong unionist who felt equally betrayed by the secessionists. Later on, as commandant of West Point, he claimed that Jefferson Davis' "parricidal hand had filled it [the Academy] with poisonous weed of succession. The depth of his treachery has not been plumbed yet..."

As the country moved toward Civil War, an equally dramatic change was occuring in Reynolds' private life. The confirmed thirty-nine-year-old bachelor met and fell in love with Catherine Mary Hewitt, a twenty-year-old Catholic girl. The details of their courtship are few, but when Reynolds was ordered east in the next year, Kate was to follow and take up residence at a Catholic School near Philadelphia. Reynolds would presumably steal some time with her when visiting nearby family. Their relationship would remain a secret to the day he died.

AGONIES OF DISSOLUTION

Reynolds obtained leave in the summer of 1860 and was able to visit his hometown before moving into his new post as Commandant of the Cadet Corps at West Point. Although he had regarded West Point as a choice duty post in 1845, by 1860 he was having his doubts: "I have not been on duty for a week trying to persuade myself that I shall like it." Given the high percentage of Southern cadets, and the high sectional tension, Reynolds had stepped into a hornet's nest, and he knew it.

Nonetheless, the duties of commandant had to be mastered, and Reynolds did his best. "These included the teaching of tactics for artillery, cavalry, and infantry; also equitation, strategy, grand tactics, and army administration." He was assisted in these chores by such future Civil War notables as Fitzhugh Lee, Charles Griffin, and Charles Field. One of his primary responsibilities while in command of the Cadet Corps was that of chief disciplinary officer, which was a difficult enough job during normal times.

Reynolds' discipline fell heavy on one cadet in particular, who watched his class leave for Washington in June 1861 from his quarters, placed there under arrest by the commandant. This young man was academically last in his class and three demerits short of expulsion, and after being brought before Reynolds for another offense, a court-martial was sought, but never obtained. Reynolds would have liked to have kicked this rascal—one George Armstrong Custer—out of the army, but hadn't the time to accomplish it. Nor was Custer the only cadet to feel the lash of discipline. Over the months Reynolds' cadets came to see him in the same tyrannical light that he had seen Commandant C.F. Smith during his own time at the Point. Not that he minded. Later, he was happy to note that, on his departure, there was "great rejoicing among the cadets at their being relieved of me."

Increasingly, Reynolds' attention was drawn to the developing national crisis. However badly his brother had managed the family estate, James was proving quite useful in bringing John's name to the attention of a fellow Pennsylvanian, Simon Cameron, the new Secretary of War. Reynolds himself was well aware that the current crisis meant fresh opportunities for promotion and advancement. He was willing to "serve in any position the government may call me to, with all the energy and power I possess." At the same time, Reynolds, the unionist, had lost all confidence in the administration of his benefactor, President James Buchanan. "...a more disgraceful plot, on the part of our friend B's cabinet officers and the leading politicians of the South, to break up our Government, has never blackened the pages of history of any nation."

In early March, Reynolds received an offer to join the staff of commanding General Winfield Scott. In making the offer, Scott noted that "several years ago I said to you that I should offer you the first vacancy for an aide de camp that might occur on my staff," remarking further that Reynolds was the only officer he would consider for the post. Naturally the West Point Commandant was flattered by the offer, but was also well aware that opportunities for wartime distinction lay not at headquarters, but in the field, and so he declined.

The attack on Fort Sumter, April 12, 1861, made the job of the academy commandant all but impossible. Reynolds assured the Southern cadets that they would be allowed the opportunity to complete their studies, at the same time speculating that by the end of April there would be no southern cadets left at West Point. On May 2 orders came to graduate the first-class cadets at once, and, somewhat amazed at the turn of events, Reynolds wondered about his own future, writing as follows: "…how long I will remain is uncertain. Much, everything, I may say depends on the turn events take, and Revolutionary events culminate rapidly…One can hardly realize that this great nation is in the agonies of dissolution."

While stationed at Fort Trumbull, just outside New London, Reynolds received another promotion and a fresh batch of orders. He received a brigadier's appointment in mid-September, back-dated to August 20, and soon after was handed a telegram from Major General George B. McClellan, commander of the Army of the Potomac: "Do you accept your appointment of brig. general and if so when will you be here—answer." As Reynolds was deliberating his promotion, another set of orders arrived assigning him to Hattaras Inlet, North Carolina, under the command of General John Wool, who was delighted to obtain the services of "such an able and experienced officer." When McClellan got wind of this he complained directly to the secretary of war. As a consequence, on September 12, Reynolds was directed to report to Washington, D.C., to the headquarters of the Army of the Potomac.

Here he was assigned the First Brigade of the Pennsylvania Reserve Division, which was commanded by General George McCall, and which consisted of the 1st, 2nd, 5th, and 8th Pennsylvania Volunteer Regiments. (The Second and Third Brigades were commanded by Brigadier General George G. Meade and Edward C. Ord, a friend from Reynolds' Rogue River days.)

Arriving on September 16, just in time to see the division mustered into federal service, Reynolds wrote home a description of his new command:

> Since I have been here I have been assigned a Brigade in McCall's Division, and rode out today to see them and the ground they are occupying, in Camp near Tenallytown, not very far from the Chain Bridge, though not on the sacred soil of Virginia, being on this side of the Potomac. I am to have the 1st Brigade.

General McClellan was determined to whip the volunteer army into shape before sending it again into action, thereby avoiding the hasty mistakes of Bull Run. Reynolds shared this philosophy and his skepticism of volunteers was reinforced in early October, when the division crossed into Virginia and his men plundered several houses left vacant by fleeing secessionists. Their commander had witnessed similar depradations in Mexico and was appalled by the volunteers. "I almost despair from what I have seen of them since I have been here."

On October 18, 1861, Reynolds made a reconaissance in the direction of Dranesville, Virginia, which resulted in a small skirmish between one of his regiments and some Louisiana Cavalry, which cost the latter one casualty. Once again Reynolds was thoroughly disgusted, writing to his sister that his men "plundered and marauded most disgracefully...I have however an officer and 3 men in arrest under charges for their plundering at Dranesville and hope to have them hung, if I can..."

He was unable to arrange a hanging, but the severity of his response made a distinct impression on his volunteers. "He used few words but with a look he could crush an offender." Another young volunteer recalled that Reynolds' "dark, piercing eyes...could burn right through a man." For himself, Reynolds decided that when he had concluded that volunteers were hopeless, he would try to return to the Fourteenth Infantry, for he was sure that he could succeed with "regulars."

Nor did the disgusted brigadier have much use for journalists: "...you need not look for...letter writing in the papers from our division for I am happy to say we are not favored with newspaper correspondents." Strange words, some would say, from the son of a former newspaper publisher and editor, but in this attitude he was at one with other "regular" officers such as William T. Sherman and John Buford. One of Reynolds staff officers recalled watching the general receive a pair of journalists coldly, and then, after directing them to apply to headquarters for information, turn his back and abruptly walk away.

Meanwhile, there was one more brief flurry of action for the Reserve Division near Dranesville. On December 20, Ord's Third Brigade engaged a mixed force of 1,200 Rebel infantry and cavalry commanded by General J.E.B. Stuart. Although Reynolds and Meade were within supporting distance, they were unable to arrive in time to participate. The whole affair lasted about an hour, with Ord winning the field, though he remained only long enough to collect his wounded before heading back to camp.

Afterwards, Reynolds wrote home critically of his brigade, stating that while he had confidence in his first and fifth regiments, they suffered like the others from the want of knowledgeable officers. And, it is significant that Reynolds cautioned his sister to keep this information to herself and not allow his letters to be shown outside the family. Clearly, there was a wariness and even secretiveness to Reynolds' personal makeup that had been reinforced by the political nature of the war and the highly politicized army atmosphere. Perhaps as a former Buchanan Democrat he wished to avoid the suspicion of disloyalty that would taint the careers of George McClellan and Fitz John Porter, fellow West Point Democrats who were publically critical of the Lincoln administration and the war effort, and who would later pay a price.

THE ARMY BEFORE RICHMOND

In the winter of 1862, the administration grew increasingly impatient with McClellan and the inactivity of the Army of the Potomac. Finally, in early February, "Little Mac" submitted a plan that called for shipping almost the entire army down the Potomac River to the Chesapeake Bay, to disembark at Fort Monroe, Virginia, on the peninsula between the York and James Rivers.

As the debate raged over the finer points of McClellan's scheme, President Lincoln took matters into his own hands and ordered the plan put into effect by March 18, 1862, but with a sufficient reserve force left before Washington, D.C., to protect it from attack. As a consequence, when the Army of the Potomac embarked to begin the Peninsula campaign, the Pennsylvania Reserves and Reynolds' Brigade were at the last moment detached and kept back to cover Washington.

Writing home on March 22, Reynolds speculated as to what the future might hold: "...we are awaiting transportation, by water, where to is not known precisely, tho somewhere from Aquia Creek to Old Point [Virginia]..." But, as events unfolded, the First Corps remained ashore and was marched instead to Fredericksburg, Virginia. Meanwhile, there came news of a great battle being fought in the West. While John Reynolds regarded Shiloh as a complete victory, he apparently had little confidence in the Federal commander: "...the surprise of an Army under Grant, is not surprising to me." Grant's pre-war reputation as a heavy drinker was not forgotten by those who had known him in the regular army.

In early May the First Corps marched into Falmouth, on the Rappahannock River, opposite Fredericksburg. Here it was directed to remain on the northern side to protect Washington not only from the Rebels to the south, but also from General Stonewall Jackson who had begun wreaking havoc among Federal forces in the Shenandoah Valley. On May 24, corps commander McDowell was ordered into the valley with two divisions, thereby leaving McCall's Division in front of Fredericksburg. Two days later, John Reynolds took his brigade across the river, occupied the town, and for two weeks became its military governor. His rule there was both firm and courteous, and the inhabitants seemed well-behaved, though Reynolds believed them to be "secesh of the first water."

While sitting in Fredericksburg, Reynolds' letters began to exhibit a certain exasperation at being left out of the war. (Finally, on June 8, 1862, the Pennsylvania Reserves were ordered to embark aboard the steamer "Cannonius" to journey to the peninsula and the seat of war.) "We have just dropped our anchor in the York River below West Point...tomorrow we will be up at the White House, where we march to join the Army before Richmond."

Reynolds' Brigade was thrown into action almost immediately upon their arrival at White House, Virginia. Two days earlier, Jeb Stuart had undertaken the reconnaissance mission that would result in his celebrated ride around McClellan's army. On the evening of June 13, he attacked Turnstall's Station, a key supply deport on the Richmond and York Railroad, and Reynolds was ordered to march to its relief. His brigade arrived around midnight, just in time to catch a wisp of Stuart's dust and to assist in extinguishing fires set by the Gray Cavalier.

Six days later, McCall's Reserves were ordered to cross the Chickahominy River and report to General Fitz John Porter, whose newly created Fifth Corps held McClellan's right flank near the town of Mechanicsville. The Pennsylvanians were positioned furthest to the right behind Beaver Dam Creek, a small stream less than a mile from town. Reynolds was given the task of constructing the divisional defense line, and Porter was highly pleased by his performance, remarking that "he had the best reasons not only to be contented but thoroughly gratified with admirable arrangements of this accomplished officer." Unquestionably, Reynolds, the seasoned artillerist, had an eye for good ground.

Following his ride around McClellan, Stuart had reported to General Robert E. Lee that the Federal right flank was up "in the air." Lee, who had earlier replaced General Joseph Johnston as Confederate commander, realized that he could save Richmond only by launching a bold offensive strike. He regarded Porter's exposed flank as a golden opportunity and devised a plan wherein he would march the bulk of his infantry to the north, while leaving a small reserve to demonstrate in front of McClellan's main force opposite the Richmond trenches. Once in position, this larger force would be joined by Jackson's 18,000-man army coming down from the Shenandoah. In combination the two would hit and roll up Porter's flank, thereby throwing the Army of the Potomac into pandemonium—assuming, of course, perfect timing all around.

The Rebel assault was scheduled to commence at dawn on June 26, with Jackson hitting from the north while three divisions struck from the south. Unfortunately, Jackson was six hours late, and upon arriving, unaccountably failed to attack. By late afternoon, division commander A.P. Hill could wait no longer for Jackson. On his own authority, the impetuous Hill launched a head-on attack against Reynolds' defenses, with such results as Reynolds recorded in his official report of August 13 (unfinished):

> The enemy appeared in force about 3:00 p.m. and opened with his batteries from the high ground around Mechanicsville. Impetuously, assailing with superior force

Brigadier General John F. Reynolds, USV. (1861)
(Courtesy Franklin and Marshall College)

> and at the same time the right and left of our position by the roads leading from that place. He was repulsed in every effort to turn our position as well as in an attempt to the right by the ford and old dam where he was handsomely checked by the 2nd Regiment.

Further in the report, for the first time, the hard-bitten "regular" waxed eloquent in praise of his Union volunteers: "The conduct of the troops, most of them for the first time under fire was all that could be desired and was creditable to their state and country..." Reynolds himself seemed to be all over the field that day, and was mentioned favorably in the dispatches of both Porter and McCall. Third Brigade commander Truman Seymour stated that "much of the credit of the day" belonged to Reynolds. Captain Evan Woodward remembered seeing him riding the lines and crying out, "Look at them, boys, in the swamp there, they are thick as flies on gingerbread; fire low, fire low."

While McClellan was pleased with the Fifth Corps performance, he realized that his right flank was still vulnerable. Furthermore, if Jackson shook off his lethargy the following day, this corps would be in serious trouble. Therefore, that night he ordered Porter to fall back four miles to Gaines Mill, a small village overlooking Boatswain's Creek. Porter, in turn, decided to put the Pennsylvania division in reserve as a reward for their fine performance of the previous day.

Lee resumed his attack at 2:00 p.m. on the following afternoon. By 4:00 p.m. the weight of Confederate numbers began to tell, and the Reserve Division was called in. Reynolds now dashed to and fro, juggling his regiments to plug whatever holes occurred in the line. Later, in his official report, Porter praised the Pennsylvania Reserves and noted that John Reynolds had acted "under a true maxim and the generous spirit of a soldier," moving to the sound of the guns, and leading his men "wherever our hardpressed forces required most assistance." The Fifth Corps was able to hold its own against vastly superior forces until about 7:00 p.m., when a Confederate brigade broke through at the center, thereby forcing a Union retreat. McClellan, now on his heels, would shift his base to Harrison's Landing on the James River. There would be hard fighting to come, but for John Reynolds, the Peninsula campaign abruptly ended with his capture on the morning of June 28. He described the episode as follows:

> After the second day's fight, I had withdrawn my brigade from the action around Gaines Mill. I went with my Adj. Gen. to the right of the line to post the artillery, or to get it changed to different position where I remained till nearly

> dark, when endeavoring to return to my brigade, I found the left of our line had given way and the Confederate pickets occupying the ground I had passed over, and taking what I thought a direct course through the woods to our rear, became entangled in the swamp with my horse wounded, and unable to extricate him, I remained there through the night, and when day broke made another effort to regain the position of our lines, but was unfortunately unsuccessful and taken prisoner.

CONFEDERATE GUEST

In all, Reynolds would spend six weeks in captivity, and in the beginning, his accommodations were quite respectable, if not luxurious. He was confined to a room at the Spotswood, one of the finer hotels in Richmond, where he even ran up a bill of $44, although it is uncertain what he received or whether he ever paid for it. Later, when more prisoners arrived, including General McCall, who was captured at the Battle of New Market Crossroads (June 30, 1862), Reynolds was transferred to a tobacco warehouse. After an escape attempt by several officers, McCall, Reynolds, and the others were marched through the streets to Libby Prison. Following his release, Reynolds had very little to say concerning his experiences as a Confederate guest. General Abner Doubleday later wrote that Reynolds "must have suffered much during his captivity, for he disliked to refer to the subject, and I remember he said that he was confined in a cell with a negro and fed on refuse food." At the time, Reynolds notified his family that he was again back under the "old flag" and that he hoped never again to be "subjected to Rebel tyranny."

Strangely enough, during this period of distasteful captivity, Reynolds received a Rebel testimonial that may have played a role in his release. Upon hearing of his imprisonment, the citizens of Fredericksburg ("secesh of the first water") had drafted a formal petition informing the Confederate government of the fair and just treatment they had received at Reynolds hands, and included a request that he be "placed on parole," if it could be done without comprising military security. Whether this petition played a role in securing Reynolds release, it certainly indicates that he was widely perceived as an officer and gentleman of the old school, a man ever respectful of the rights of private citizens.

When Reynolds and McCall arrived at army headquarters at Harrison's Landing on August 13, the Pennsylvania Reserves lined up to greet them, cheering wildly. Unquestionably, a bond of affection and respect had been forged between Reynolds and his men at Mechanicsville and Gainesville. Despite his aloof exterior, the men had witnessed his valor and competence under fire and had responded in kind. Reynolds' pride in his brigade was revealed in his official report, and one of his aides, Charles Lamborn, wrote the Reynolds sisters that: "His whole brigade is most decidedly attached to him, and I do not think the love of any commander was ever felt more deeply or sincerely than his."

NORTH TO MANASSAS

Soon after, General McCall returned home in ill health and John Reynolds assumed command of the Pennsylvania Reserves, mustering now only 7,000 effectives.

Meanwhile, during Reynolds' absence the strategic picture had changed radically. At the conclusion of the Seven Days Battles, on July 1, Lee had accomplished his mission of driving McClellan from the gates of Richmond. From his base at Harrison's Landing, McClellan blamed the Lincoln administration for withholding troops and called for reinforcement. There followed an impasse of several days before the administration, in exasperation, ordered "Little Mac" to re-embark his army and steam north to reinforce General John Pope, who had been brought from the west to command the newly designated Army of Virginia, some 56,000 strong, in the Shenandoah.

In retaliation, McClellan went into a sulk and took his sweet time in re-embarking the Army of the Potomac. Observing the Federal disarray from Richmond, Robert E. Lee saw an opportunity to bag Pope's army before the tardy McClellan could reassemble his. Lee sent Jackson's Corps north in mid-August and then, once he was certain that Richmond was safe, followed with Longstreet's Corps. The Peninsula campaign was over; the Second Manassas campaign had just begun.

Ordered north in support, Reynolds' Pennsylvania Division arrived at Rappahannock Station near Pope's headquarters on August 22. Not that Reynolds particularly cared for the movement or the political motives behind it: "I do not approve of the operation of leaving the line of the James River, to be sure I do not take political projects into consideration." He would sound this theme again and again, though circumspectly, and only in letters home. In Reynolds' mind, politics and war were separate entities and he believed that politicians should never influence or dictate the movements of armies. Still, he seemed resigned to the fact—"…I suppose they [political considerations] will have, as they have heretofore, overruled all military ones."

By August 28, Pope had concentrated his army around Warrenton, Virginia. Two days earlier "Stonewall" Jackson had marched through Thoroughfare Gap, and the next day seized Pope's supply depot at Manassas Junction. In response, Pope chose to move toward Manassas, but by then, Jackson had abandoned the depot and moved down the Warrenton Turnpike to await him near the village of Groveton. As Reynolds marched up the turnpike on the morning of the 28th, his division brushed up against Jackson's men, and he prepared to go after them. A private in the ranks remembered seeing the general riding among the troops: "…and with soldierly coolness and courage, he proceeded to arrange a line of battle." But, the Pennsylvania Reserves were now attached to McDowell's Third Corps of the Army of Virginia, and McDowell's intelligence placed Jackson at Manassas, not Groveton. Therefore, Reynolds was instructed to disengage and continue his march.

Very quickly, Pope's army began to unravel in confusion. Jackson was next reported to be at Centreville in force, though this force was only a single division commanded by A.P. Hill. As Reynolds' Reserves moved out, heavy firing could be heard in the direction of Groveton, where General John Gibbon's "Black Hat Brigade" had engaged Jackson's men in a savage fight that would result in over a thousand combined casualties. Reynolds spun about and spurred his mount toward Groveton, arriving there just as the fighting subsided. Realizing that the force he had earlier bumped against was indeed Jackson's, Reynolds urged Gibbon's division commander, General Rufus King, to hold his ground, on the promise that Reynolds would bring his reserve division up in support the following morning. Unfortunately, later that evening, King had a change of heart and decided to withdraw.

Reynolds would find the next day, August 29, equally as frustrating. That morning, believing that he had Jackson on the run, Pope attempted to pull his army together for a concerted attack near the old Bull Run Battlefield. Unfortunately, unbeknownst to Pope, that afternoon Lee had arrived with Longstreet's Corps on his extreme left flank. Giving little thought to his left, Pope continued to assault Jackson's Corps, though without much success. In his mind, the left flank would be handled by Fitz John Porter's Fifth Corps, which was supposedly marching up in support via the Manassas-Gainesville Road.

The following day, Pope ordered his troops north of the pike to advance, while to the south he expected the Fifth Corps to move up with Reynolds' Reserves in support on Porter's extreme left. Incredibly, Pope then misinterpreted Longstreet's re-shuffling of his corps as the beginning of a general Confederate retreat. Porter got his corps moving by mid-afternoon, but met with stiff resistance, and John Reynolds found the going especially rough. When his skirmishers began falling back on his own extreme left, Reynolds rode over and testily inquired as to the reason. Informed of a heavy concentration of Rebels, he rode on to see for himself, and was stunned by the sight of a line of skirmishers with cavalry behind it, "...evidently masking a column of the enemy formed for an attack on my left." As Reynolds spun round, he was the target of a Rebel volley which killed one of his orderlies. Riding on, he reported this news at McDowell's headquarters and was ordered to pull his division back to Chinn Ridge covering the Warrenton Turnpike. One unsubstantiated story has it that Reynolds also went directly to Pope, only to have the latter discount his report of Longstreet's presence with the remark saying: "Oh I guess not." In any case, Reynolds' Division now had the task of covering the Union left against Longstreet's entire corps.

Porter was able to put up stiff resistance, but eventually the weight of Longstreet's attack caused the Fifth Corps to collapse. Reynolds' Division watched as Porter's men broke for the rear, and prepared for the coming onslaught. Just then, Reynolds received orders to march to the rear of the fleeing Fifth Corps in an attempt to rally them, which proved impossible. He was next ordered to Henry House Hill, where Pope was assembling a force to protect his line of retreat. This eminence became a key position as Longstreet pushed to the Warrenton/Sudley Road junction, in hopes of cutting Pope in half. Only the obstinate stand by Reynolds' Division and other Union troops near Henry House Hill enabled Pope to save his army that day.

At one point, as a Confederate brigade presented an open flank to the Pennsylvanians, Reynolds grasped the flag of the Second Reserves, waved it aloft, shouted "Forward Reserves!", and led a downhill charge which stopped the Rebels in their tracks. Later, when his division showed signs of breaking, Reynolds seized the flag of the 6th Reserves, and rode up and down the line to steady it. In these moments he made himself such an easy mark for sharpshooters that one of his men thought that the general led a "charmed life." Such performances were becoming common with John Reynolds, and his heroism on Henry House Hill helped prevent Lee from converting a stunning victory into a staggering defeat for the Union cause.

RETURN OF McCLELLAN

Pope's army held until nearly dusk, and Reynolds' Reserves were some of the last regiments to leave the field. Fortunately, the Confederates were near exhaustion themselves and unable to mount a determined pursuit. Their victory, however, meant the end of General John Pope, who was transferred to the Minnesota Indian frontier, all the while protesting that he had been the victim of a conspiracy. He did, however, have words of high praise for a few, which included John Reynolds and the officers of the Reserves, "...who performed their duties with ability and gallantry and in all fidelity to the Government and to the army." In light of their later association at Gettysburg, it is significant that cavalryman John Buford received praise similar to Reynolds.

On September 2, President Lincoln ordered McClellan to assume command of all federal forces in the East and to prepare to defend the capital. By then, however, Lee had opted for another plan. Having suffered heavy casualties himself, the Gray Fox realized that his army lacked the strength to overcome the Washington fortifications. Unwilling to sacrifice the offensive momentum he had gained, he decided instead to invade Maryland. By September 6, 1862, his intentions were becoming clear to a number of Union officers, including John Reynolds, who wrote..."I do not know what the [Rebel] movement portends except the enemy are evidently bent on an invasion of the North."

In McClellan's reorganization of the army, the Reserves were assigned to the First Army Corps under Major General Joe Hooker. The division had earned a reputation as a hard fighting unit, and its assignment to Hooker's Corps meant further opportunity to excel. Unfortunately, John Reynolds would not be available to share the opportunity, for at the same time that Lee led his army into Maryland, Reynolds was relieved of command and ordered to Pennsylvania, at the request of Governor Andrew Curtain.

When it became apparent that his state was in danger, Curtin had requested the return of the Pennsylvania Reserve Division to Harrisburg. The War Department refused to comply, assuring the governor that the Reserves could better serve Pennsylvania by remaining with the Army of the Potomac. In lieu of the Reserves, Curtin requested "an active energetic officer to command the forces in the field and one that could rally Pennsylvania. It is believed that General Reynolds would be most as useful." After much wrangling between Harrisburg and Washington, the governor got his general and Reynolds, much to his disgust, was ordered to Harrisburg.

He arrived on September 13, set up headquarters at the state capital, and got down to the task of whipping the assembled mob into some semblance of a force that might fight. The situation was grim, and his letter to family was scarcely reassuring:

> I think the threatening aspect of an invasion down the Cumberland Valley very serious, there is nothing to prevent their doing great injury, and in fact their marching to this place a well organized column of 20 or 30,000 men, cavalry and infantry, etc.; there is nothing in the valley to stop them.

Characteristically, he added a footnote to the letter, instructing his sister to "Burn this up and do not let anyone see it..." As events unfolded, there was very little that Reynolds could do about anything, for his state militia would refuse to cross into Maryland. In the next two weeks, while the Battles of South Mountain and Antietam were being fought, the commander of the Pennsylvania Militia would go no further south than Chambersburg. As for Antietam, in Reynolds' view, "we rather had the advantage...though not much to boast of." Following Lee's retreat back into Virginia, he was permitted to disband the militia and return to the army, much to his relief. The militia wanted to defend their homes, he later wrote, but "they preferred to wait until the enemy actually reached their own door steps before they encountered him."

Upon return, Reynolds found himself in temporary charge of the First Corps, assuming command from General George Meade, who had led the corps since General Hooker's wounding at Antietam. As highly ambitious as Reynolds, and just as circumspect, Meade wrote to his wife that he wished Reynolds "would have stayed away." But, as an old army "regular" himself, Meade accepted the seniority system and would "subside gracefully into a division commander." Though the rivalry between these two would intensify as their stars began to rise, they were also developing a mutual respect that was rare among backbiting Federal corps commanaders.

Following his narrow victory at Antietam, McClellan decided to refit and rebuild his army, much to the dismay of President Lincoln, who hoped that he would vigorously pursue Lee and bring him to battle before winter set in. Tensions escalated and by early November the President had enough of "Little Mac." On November 7, he was sacked for good and replaced as commander of the Army of the Potomac by Major General Ambrose Burnside, a meager talent at best.

In the meanwhile, Reynolds was becoming acquainted with his new corps. At a review held on October 2, he believed that the men demonstrated little enthusiasm, but one of them noted that Reynolds was "alertness personified." His artillery chief, Colonel Charles Wainwright, observed that the general "shows to advantage" on horseback, in one instance riding down a steep hill at such a rate that only a few of the staff could keep up. John Reynolds would command this corps to the end of his life, and take as much pride in his men as they did in him. As one volunteer put it: "To the First Corps General Reynolds was the 'beau ideal' of a soldier."

"I HAVE HARD WORK AHEAD OF ME"

The removal of McClellan was a great shock to the army, and in Reynolds' view the dismissal had been "unwise, injudicious, as it was uncalled for." Nonetheless, he was happy to write that McClellan's departure caused less ill will than he had feared, and that all must pull together in support of Burnside, who was "as noble a spirit as ever existed." Not everyone shared Reynolds' estimate of Burnside, but it is worth noting that Reynolds could always look past his own ambition and wholeheartedly support whomever commanded the army.

Burnside was now under extreme pressure from the administration to engage Lee before winter set in, and at least initially he seemed up to the task. He submitted a plan for a rapid march around Lee's right flank at Culpeper, with the aim of occupying Fredericksburg so as to threaten Richmond from the north. Lincoln was reluctant to agree, feeling that Lee's army should be the target, not Richmond. Burnside set the Army of the Potomac quickly in motion on November 15, and had his leading elements in position on the Rappahannock River opposite Fredericksburg by the 18th. Pontoons were required to transport the army across, but unfortunately the orders for them had gone astray. By the time the pontoons did arrive on November 25, Lee had occupied the town and begun to fortify the heights commanding it.

Previously, the army had been reorganized into three "Grand Divisions" consisting of two corps apiece. Reynolds' First Corps, along with General William F. Smith's Sixth Corps, made up the "Left Grand Division," while the Third and Fifth Corps made up the "Center Grand Division," and the Second and Ninth Corps the "Right Grand Division." By the end of November, Franklin's Grand Division had been positioned along the river to the east of town, with Reynolds' First Corps posted on the extreme left flank. While awaiting further orders, on December 2, Reynolds received his commission as major general, backdated to November 29.

Finally, on the evening of December 10, the First Corps was ordered to march to the river and prepare to cross while, early on the 11th, engineers

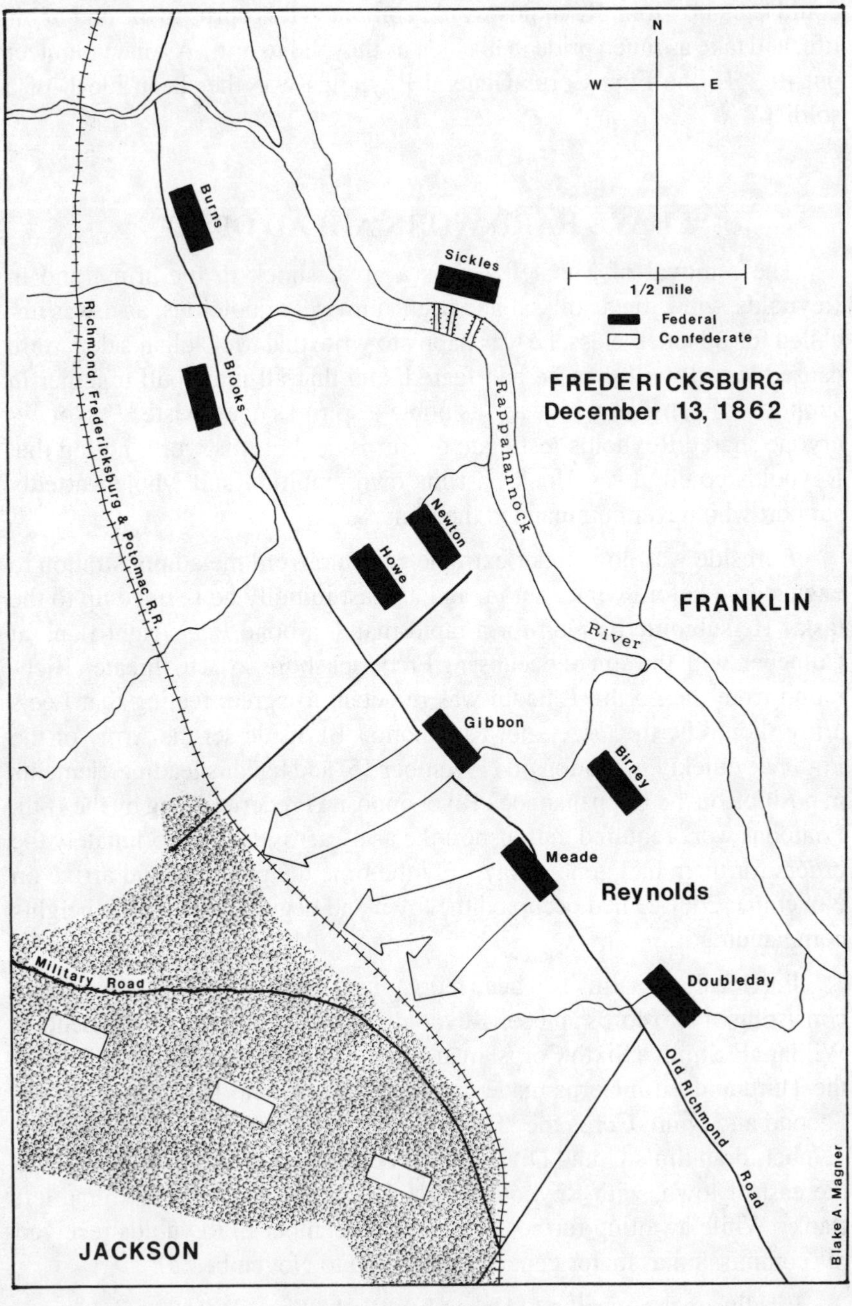

N
W
E
1/2 mile
Federal
Confederate
FREDERICKSBURG
December 13, 1862
Burns
Sickles
Brooks
Richmond, Fredericksburg & Potomac R.R.
Rappahannock
River
Newton
Howe
FRANKLIN
Gibbon
Birney
Meade
Reynolds
Doubleday
Military Road
Old Richmond Road
JACKSON
Blake A. Magner

began the construction of pontoon bridges. Rebel snipers, however, slowed the operation considerably and the crossing was held up until the following afternoon. Further up river, the remainder of the army was having even greater difficulty; their pontoons would not be in place until late afternoon on December 11.

Grand Division Commander Franklin established his headquarters in a house owned by a man whom Reynolds had known during his own previous occupation of Fredericksburg. This gentleman, one Mr. Bernard, presented himself as a Union man, but the First Corps commander knew better, and had him arrested and unceremoniously escorted across the river. General Franklin later observed that "Reynolds on such occasions was a man of few words."

Franklin, Reynolds, and Smith concurred that an all-out assault with their entire force (two corps, three divisions each) was the only way to carry the heights to their front. They presented this plan to Burnside later in the day and he seemed to agree. The three generals waited that night at headquarters, but no orders came, and by 3:00 a.m. Reynolds could wait no longer. "I know I have hard work ahead of me and I must get some sleep."

"ALMOST GAINING THE OBJECTIVE"

Orders reached Franklin at 7:30 a.m., December 13, but they were not what he had expected. Instead of a concentrated, all-out assault, Franklin was directed to attack with a division "at least" and seize the heights near Hamilton's Crossing. Reynolds' Corps was chosen to make the assault, and Reynolds selected his most trusted division—Meade's 4,000-man Pennsylvania Reserves—as the spearhead to lead it. A dense fog covered the Reserves as they moved across the Old Richmond Road to form a line of battle. The Confederates on the heights opposite Meade's troops, men of Jackson's Corps, could hear the sounds of their approach, but it was not until 10:00 a.m. that the fog lifted and presented the spectacle of the entire Left Grand Division. George Meade, the point commander, was supported by Doubleday's Division to the left, and Gibbon's to his right.

It was nearly noon by the time that Meade had everyone in position, but unfortunately, one of Reynolds' former West Point cadets managed to mischievously prolong the business. Just as Meade was preparing to step off, Major John Pelham of Stuart's Confederate Horse Artillery posted two guns on the Old Richmond Road and opened up, thereby scattering troops and prompting further delay.

Meade finally attacked at 1:00 p.m., though without the support of Doubleday, who now had to guard against Confederates on the left. The Reserves charged through the woods at the base of the hills and on up the heights, finding a gap in Jackson's line, and causing two Rebel brigades to fall back. The division next slammed into a brigade of South Carolinians, scattering them while killing their commander, General Maxcy Gregg. By now, however, Meade's troops were winded and desperately in need of support. Observing this, Reynolds ordered Gibbon to get his division moving, but despite his support the Reserves were forced to retreat.

Unfortunately, the business of getting out proved much more difficult than getting in. Meade was unable to form an effective rearguard on the downhill slopes and the division began to break apart. Reynolds and Meade worked feverishly to rally them behind the artillery near the Old Richmond Road, and Franklin was able to bring up enough supports to make the Confederates think twice about pressing their advantage. Furious at having received so little support during his attack, Meade rode up to his commander and exclaimed, "My God, General Reynolds, did they think my division could whip Lee's whole army?!" Although the Pennsylvania Reserves did not do all the fighting on the left, they certainly carried the heaviest load, suffering forty percent casualties. Their brief success proved to be the only bright spot in a very dark day for the Federals, as brigades of the other grand divisions battered themselves in futile assaults against "Marye's Heights."

Reynolds took a few moments that evening to write and give the home front some idea of the "...events of the past few days." He criticized the tactics of the entire campaign, and believed that Franklin had interpreted his orders too narrowly. He was also surprisingly critical of his own First Corps:

> My Corps, or two Divisions of it made the attack on the left and after almost gaining the object let it slip. They did not do as well as I expected tho' they advanced under Artillery fire very well. When it came to the attack of the wooded heights they faltered and failed—we are fortunate that it is not worse.

The total Federal casualties were appalling; some 12,000 Union soldiers fell on a single day. Talked out of continuing the slaughter the next day, Burnside ordered a withdrawal to commence on the evening of the 15th. Straw was placed on the bridges to deaden the sound, and Reynolds himself rode the picket lines to make sure the evacuation was carried out quietly.

Burnside now began the process of identifying those officers responsible for his defeat, and in mid-January, after another failed offensive which became known as Burnside's "Mud March," he demanded the dismissal of his enemies, which by now included most of the Union high command. Looking on in dismay, Reynolds wrote home to say that "if we do not get someone who can command an Army without consulting 'Stanton and Halleck' at Washington, I do not know what will become of this army." In the end, the Lincoln administration allowed Sumner to resign, dismissed Franklin and Burnside, and appointed "Fighting Joe" Hooker as commander of the Army of the Potomac. Once again, Reynolds had survived a bloodletting of the top command with his reputation intact. Indeed, he had not only survived, but his own claim to the top command had grown stronger. In the midst of dismal failure, his star was on the rise.

In the winter of 1863, Hooker began the monumental task of rebuilding the army, now at its lowest ebb since Pope's debacle the previous August. He junked the "Grand Divisions," instituted some crucial reforms affecting health and sanitation, set up a furlough system, and began enforcing strict discipline in camp. Lincoln came to review the army in early April and Reynolds believed that the President was "much gratified with all he saw." He went on to quote Lincoln as saying that "if the troops only fight as well as they looked no expectations, however great, need be disappointed." Reynolds himself was optimistic and felt the army "with proper management...will achieve a success undoubtedly."

"THEY GOT MORE OF THE SPOILS"

In the spring campaign to come, Hooker planned to hold Lee below Fredericksburg with three Federal corps, while sneaking up river to cross and come down on the Confederate left flank with the remainder of his army.

Reynolds' First Corps was assigned to the Fredericksburg wing, which included the Third and Sixth Corps, under the overall command of General John Sedgwick. On the morning of April 28, as Hooker moved north, Sedgwick ordered Reynolds to move his corps down near the Rappahannock crossing, taking special care to keep his men concealed. As night fell, Chief Engineer Henry Benham began laying the bridges, but quickly fell behind schedule. Reynolds' nerves became exceptionally taut, and a staff member observed that he "swore pretty hard when things did not go to suit him." His composure received an extra jolt when a noticeably drunk Benham rode up, face bleeding from an accident, and loudly cried out,

"Hurrah Josh, Hurrah for here and Buena Vista!" By now, the Confederates realized that something was up and began firing from the opposite bank, but Reynolds decided to wait until day before making any sudden moves.

A low fog hung close to the ground that morning of the 29th as Reynolds and his First Division commander, General James Wadsworth, sat on horseback, smoking cigars, gazing across the Rappahannock. When the fog lifted Wadsworth was ordered to send two regiments across the river to clear out enemy snipers; by late afternoon Reynolds had put two divisions across on the Fredericksburg side. Despite the delay, all was going tolerably well along Sedgwick's front.

Unfortunately, the same could not be said for Joe Hooker. After a promising start, in which his men had marched quickly, crossed the river, and come down on Lee's flank, "Fighting Joe" began to lose his nerve. Just when his plan was working well, Hooker ordered a halt, and then a withdrawal to the little crossroads known as Chancellorsville. That night John Reynolds wrote home praising the recent developments, but was still a bit uneasy: "The only thing I do not like about our operations has been that the bridges were thrown to soon here by a day." His fears were well gounded. By the evening of the 30th, Lee realized that Sedgwick's movements were merely a feint, and that Hooker's 70,000-man force around Chancellorsville was the main thrust.

Leaving but a single division in Sedgwick's front, Lee moved the remainder of his army, some 40,000 strong, to the west to confront Hooker, who by now had gone entirely on the defensive. On the evening of May 1, 1863, Lee and Jackson formulated a plan of attack that would seal the doom of "Fighting Joe." They would divide their inferior force and Jackson would march his 25,000-man corps around Hooker's right flank, while Lee held his front with the remaining 14,000. And, the plan worked almost to perfection. The following morning, Jackson marched out to circle round and at 5:00 p.m. delivered an attack that shattered the Federal Eleventh Corps and all but cut off the Union army from the river.

Somewhat earlier the nervous Hooker had ordered the Third and First Corps to come from Fredericksburg to his assistance. Reynolds' First Corps arrived at around 6:30 p.m., just in time to reinforce the collapsing Federal right, and to provide stability as Jackson's attack sputtered in the darkness. (Jackson himself was mistakenly fired upon by his own men, and was to die of wound complications eight days later.)

On May 3, Jackson's Confederates resumed their attack under the command of Jeb Stuart. Anchoring the Federal right, Reynolds and Fifth Corps commander George Meade watched in amazement as Hooker allowed Stuart to assault his center without calling on the First and Fifth Corps for assistance. Indeed, Hooker refused their requests to join in. The following day brought more of the same as Hooker, feeling the effects of a near miss by a cannonball, ordered Sedgwick's lone corps to carry the heights beyond Fredericksburg and then come to his rescue. Sedgwick made a valiant effort but was fortunate merely to escape back across the Rappahannock with his corps intact, and never mind Joe Hooker.

John Reynolds was by now furious at the inactivity issuing from Hooker's headquarters. In the hope of getting his First Corps into the fight—any kind of fight—he selected a brigade under Colonel Roy Stone and sent it out on "reconnaissance," fully expecting the fiery Stone to get into the kind of trouble that would require Reynolds to swoop in with the First Corps to rescue him. Stone pushed forward, brushed back Stuart's pickets, but upon encountering a heavier force, pulled back in the belief that he had accomplished what his general intended. When later told that the colonel could have gotten into a fight, Reynolds exclaimed, "I wish to God he had!"

On May 4, in the late evening, General Hooker called a conference of corps commanders to discuss the advisability of retreat. After reviewing the situation, Hooker excused himself to let his commanders come to a vote. Generals Meade and O.O. Howard voted to stand and fight; Generals Sickles and Couch voted for withdrawal; General Slocum was not present. John Reynolds agreed with Meade, but, since his corps had seen little action, felt reluctant to press his opinion. Having had his say, Reynolds lay down in a corner of the room to catch some sleep. Upon his return, despite the 3 to 2 vote to remain, Hooker announced the retreat, much to the irritation of Reynolds, who was heard to remark, loud enough for Hooker to hear: "What was the use of calling us together at this time of night when he intended to retreat anyhow?" This remark was as close to personal insubordination as John Reynolds would come in the whole of his military life.

By May 6, the army had re-crossed the Rappahannock and John Reynolds was in a foul mood. Visiting his headquarters during this period, General John Gibbon recalled that Reynolds "was the picture of woe and disgust and said plainly that we had been badly out-generaled and whipped by half our number." Completely discouraged, Reynolds wrote home expressing his bewilderment at a campaign that had begun so gloriously and ended so badly: "We did not effect much more by our crossing than to be slaughtered and to slaughter the Rebels. I think it will turn out that they got more of the spoils than we did."

Through the remainder of May the Army of the Potomac nursed its wounds, pulled itself together, and listened to gossip concerning the removal of Joe Hooker. Rumor had it that John Reynolds was being considered for the top job, and the rumors were on target. During its first few years, the eastern army had experienced incredible turmoil as Lincoln groped frantically for an army commander that could get the job done. In a ruthless winnowing process, army, corps, and division commanders had come and gone, some in disgrace, others shipped out to backwaters where they could do no harm. In the Union West a similar winnowing had taken place, and out there the makings of a winning command combination—Grant and Sherman, with George Thomas and Phil Sheridan in the wings—was becoming discernable. In the eastern theatre where Union forces had almost always lost, the situation was more fluid. Even so, a number of younger men were coming to the fore—Winfield Scott Hancock, George Gordon Meade, John Buford—men who would make their mark in the coming campaign. As army commander, by late May, John Reynolds had emerged as the Lincoln administration's candidate in reserve.

On May 31, Reynolds took leave and traveled to Washington, where, on June 2, he had a lengthy discussion with the President concerning the leadership of the Army of the Potomac. The man whom Hooker had called "the ablest officer under me" was now very candid in discussing his superior's strengths and weaknesses. When sounded out himself on assuming command of the army, Reynolds replied that unless he was given free rein, he would prefer to decline it.

In retrospect, it is somewhat amazing that Reynolds was offered this command. For one thing, he was junior to corps commanders Sedgwick and Slocum. For another, he was a lifelong Democrat whose military career and advancement had been due, in part, to the patronage of one of the most vilified of Democrats, James Buchanan. Then too, although Reynolds had been extremely circumspect, he was widely perceived as a McClellan man (as indeed he was) and that alone was enough to bring a lesser man down. On the other hand, Reynolds' performance at brigade, divisional, and corps level had always been solid, if not sterling. That he possessed energy, intelligence, courage, and presence was obvious to all who met him. Moreover, he was a team player who had always served loyally under whomever he was placed. Lincoln undoubtedly sensed that Reynolds' primary loyalties were to the army and the Union, however much he might disagree with the policies of a Republican administration. In rejecting command of the Army of the Potomac, Reynolds was declining the chance of a lifetime, the capstone of a career. That he chose to do so on principle is yet another measure of his character.

A rare and believed never before published photograph of General Reynolds in civilian clothes. Believed to have been taken in winter or spring of 1863.
(Courtesy Franklin and Marshall College)

Leaving that night to return to the army, Reynolds stopped in Baltimore to visit his sisters, to whom he divulged the substance of his Presidential interview. It is significant that he would also inform George Meade, but no one else. One can only guess at his state of mind. Perhaps in the wake of the interview he felt even more frustrated. Then again, perhaps he experienced a curious sense of release.

On June 12, General Hooker issued orders to set the Army of the Potomac in pursuit of Lee, who had earlier put his own army in motion to invade Pennsylvania. Ewell's was the first Confederate Corps to move via the Shenandoah Valley; A.P. Hill and Longstreet's Corps were still in the vicinity of Fredericksburg and Union intelligence had yet to figure the direction of Ewell's movements. On that day Reynolds received notice that he was to temporarily command the "right wing" of the army, consisting of his own First Corps, Meade's Fifth Corps, and Howard's Eleventh Corps. This wing was to shadow the Confederates heading north and Reynolds was instructed to keep his force between them and Washington. On June 15, 1863, Ewell attacked and seized Winchester, Virginia, capturing the Federal garrison. In the meantime, Lee put the remainder of his army on the march, ordering Hill and Longstreet into the Shenandoah in Ewell's wake. As it became obvious that Lee's objective was something other than Washington, Hooker now had to play catch up. For the men in ranks, this meant two weeks of forced marches in choking dust and stifling heat.

Reynolds' command of the Union "right wing" lasted until June 16, when Hooker moved his headquarters north to Fairfax Station. The army commander was now reduced to issuing orders calculated to keep the Army of the Potomac between the Rebels and Washington, as he searched for some clue to Lee's design. During this period he fought constantly with the adminstration, and the relation had become so strained as to make a change of command almost inevitable. Unfortunately for Hooker, Lee, too, was feeling his way, as is indicated by his June 22 orders to Richard Ewell—as Ewell crossed into Pennsylvania he was to let his "progress and direction" be shaped by the "developments and circumstances." By June 22, John Reynolds was as befuddled as Joe Hooker, writing home that "it is almost impossible to say where the enemy is with any certainty."

On June 25, Reynolds was ordered to assume command of the "left" Union wing, consisting of the First, Third, and Eleventh Corps. General Doubleday met Reynolds that day at a Potomac River crossing, and later described him as feeling "that it was necessary to attack the enemy at once, to prevent his plundering the whole state...He seemed to think if he could meet them with the First Corps there would be no doubt of the result."

On the same day that Reynolds assumed command of the "left wing," Ewell marched his corps out of Chambersburg, and accompanied two of his divisions to Harrisburg, while a third under General Jubal Early moved east toward York. Early brushed aside a regiment of militia west of Gettysburg and occupied the town on the 26th, but stayed only long enough to demand provisions, and when these were not forthcoming, moved through York to the banks of the Susquehanna the following day. He would have crossed the river and occupied Lancaster had the local militia not set fire to the bridge. As fate would have it, one of the militia soldiers was James Reynolds, John's youngest brother, who would remain with his company until July 2, when word reached him of his brother's fate.

On June 28, Abraham Lincoln relieved Joe Hooker and *ordered* General George Gordon Meade to assume command of the Army of the Potomac. Meade protested to the War Department courier that the army was expecting Reynolds, but finally accepted with the remark: "Well, I've been tried and condemned without a hearing, and I suppose I shall have to go to execution." Upon hearing of Meade's promotion, Reynolds dressed in his best uniform and went to his headquarters to pay his respects.

In this meeting, he found Meade anxious to talk to the man he considered "a lieutenant important to me in his services—a friend and a brother." The new commander went on to say how unwelcome the orders were, how he wished the position had been given to Reynolds, and how important it was to him to receive Reynolds' support at this critical time. In his turn, Reynolds assured Meade that the command had gone to the right man and that Meade could rely on him to support to the best of his ability, and with that the two generals mapped out plans to bring Lee to battle. On June 30, wing commander Reynolds, traveling with the First Corps, moved from Emmitsburg, Maryland into Pennsylvania and in mid-afternoon went into camp near Marsh Creek while setting up headquarters at the Moritz Tavern, some six miles south of Gettysburg. By now he was receiving a steady stream of information from John Buford, his cavalry commander, which he forwarded on to Meade and other pertinent commanders. "Buford sends reliable information that the enemy occupies Chambersburg in force, and that they are moving down from Cashtown." Somewhat later: "Buford is in Gettysburg, and found a regiment of Rebel infantry advancing on the town, which retired as he advanced..."— this from a dispatch sent to Howard in Emmitsburg, whom Reynolds instructed to be prepared to move "to his [Reynolds'] left, in case they move on him from Fairfield [Pennsylvania] and the mountain roads."

He spent the remainder of the day studying a variety of reports as he attempted to piece together Lee's intentions. Testimony from two different sources indicate that Reynolds experienced something of a mood swing between late afternoon and midnight. One of Meade's staff officers, visiting in the afternoon, recalled "his calm dignity, and true soldierly appearance as he courteously rose to receive me." General Howard, the Eleventh Corps commander, arrived late in the evening, and, after a light supper, joined Reynolds in pouring over the maps and messages. As they did so, Howard noticed that his commander seemed depressed. Before going to sleep Reynolds sent Meade a message summarizing all the information he had received that day, along with his opinion that in the event of a defensive battle, a position north of Emmitsburg was the place to make a stand, but that Meade should consider this opinion as mere "surmise." If Reynolds was reeling somewhat from the immense responsibility of his position, John Buford's 10:30 p.m. dispatch certainly must have increased his anxiety:

> I am satisfied that A.P. Hill's corps is massed just back of Cashtown, about nine miles from this place. Pender's division of this [Hill] corps came up today, of which I advised you, 'saying the enemy in my front was increased'. The enemy's pickets, infantry and artillery, are within four miles of this place, at the Cashtown Road...Ewell's corps is crossing the mountains from Carlisle...Longstreet, from all I can learn, is still behind Hill.

Buford concluded his dispatch with a request for instructions: "Should I have to fall back, advise me by what route." Lying on the floor of the tavern, his mind teeming with possibilities, John Reynolds undoubtedly recalled one key passage from an earlier Meade dispatch: "...If they advance against me, I must concentrate at that point where they show the strongest force."

"WHAT'S THE MATTER, JOHN?"

At approximately 4:00 a.m., July 1, 1863, the General awakened Staff Officer Stephen Weld, "as he frequently had to do," and then turned to the First Corps, instructing Wadsworth at Marsh Creek to put his division on the road to Gettysburg. Observing Reynolds that morning, Colonel Wainwright noted that though "Doubleday is supposed to be in command of our troops [First Corps], all our orders came from Reynolds direct." Obviously, where Reynolds and the First Corps were concerned, old command habits died hard. He then ordered Doubleday to follow Wadsworth with his remaining divisions while sending a message confirming Howard's order to march in support of the First Corps, and instructing him where to place his own Eleventh Corps outside of town. Word was also sent to Third Corps commander Dan Sickles to verify his movement north of Emmitsburg. To most observers, this flurry of orders and messages conveyed a crackling sense of urgency, and yet, when asked of the prospects of a fight, Reynolds replied to staff officer: "...that we were only moving to within supporting distance of Buford."

After signing all messages and paperwork, and after superintending all movements, Reynolds decided to accompany Wadsworth and rode to the head of the column, pausing only to confer before riding on. As he approached Gettysburg, Reynolds began to hear the faint sound of guns and soon met a courier from Buford with word that the Rebels were advancing on the Cashtown Road. He immediately sent Wadsworth an order to close up and hurry his column forward, and then put the spurs to "Fancy," his black stallion, and galloped toward town. Artillerist Reynolds had an eye for good ground, and as he rode up the Emmitsburg Pike he must have noticed the ridge anchored by two large hills to the east of the road. Still in the dark as to Buford's situation and the size of the force confronting him, Reynolds would have been looking for an appropriate place to position the First Corps in the event of withdrawal, and this ground from East Cemetery Hill to the Round Tops undoubtedly caught his eye.

About a half mile from town Reynolds encountered a civilian looking quite distressed, and when he inquired as to the reason, was told of the cavalry fight to the west of town. Riding on, he stopped at a house to inquire the way to Buford's headquarters at the Eagle Hotel. From there he rode into the town square and west on Chambersburg Street. Standing near the hotel that morning, Gettysburg resident Robert McClean recalled seeing Reynolds and his staff ride up to inquire about Buford. Further down, on the Chambersburg Pike, a young boy—one Daniel Skelly—saw a general mount the ridge and then ride down a lane toward the Lutheran Seminary. Reynolds galloped up to the Seminary at approximately 9:30 a.m. and shouted up to Buford in the cupola of one of the buildings, "What's the matter, John?!" The cavalry commander yelled down, "The devil's to pay!"

As the two rode out to examine Buford's position, the latter apprised Reynolds of the situation, reporting that he had been fighting nearly since dawn against Henry Heth's Division of Hill's Corps, and that his scouts reported the advance of Ewell's Corps from the north.

Reynolds was now to make a momentous decision, the most important of his life. Should he commit his 8,000-man First Corps against heavy, soon-to-be-overwhelming odds? If so, where should he position them?

Should he assume Buford's place to the west and try to save the town, or should he abandon it to occupy and fortify the heights that he had seen to the south on the Emmitsburg Road? Very quickly he decided that he would join Buford in an attempt to save the town, reasoning that at the very least he could hold long enough to allow Meade to seize the heights to the south.

Reynolds and Buford "talked for two or three minutes" by the side of the road, and then Buford was given orders to stand and continue to hold his position. Reynolds then turned to his staff. To Captain Weld he said, "Weld, I am going to pick you out to go to General Meade with a message." He was to tell the army commander that the enemy were coming in strong force, that Reynolds was afraid that the enemy would reach the heights on the other side of town before he could, and that he would fight them all through town, and hold out as long as possible! With a sense of urgency, he ordered the captain to ride fast and hard and even kill his horse if necessary to reach Meade. Reynolds also sent messages to Howard and Sickles to come to Gettysburg with all dispatch, and then sent an aide into town to advise the civilians to stay in their homes.

The wing commander now knew that he was in a race and that time was of the essence. Riding back to hurry Wadsworth's Division along, he became momentarily lost on a Gettysburg side street, but resident Catherine Foster, standing in her balcony, pointed the way to the Emmitsburg Road. In departing, Reynolds requested she go to her cellar. Soon after, he arrived on the road near the Codori Farm and directed his escort to begin tearing down the fences lining the road.

While there, he was met by Major Henry Tremain of Dan Sickles' staff, who had come looking for orders. After receiving them, the major stood listening as Reynolds gazed at Cemetery Ridge and said, "That would be a good place...but I would like to save the town. If I form there it might destroy the town. But I doubt if I shall have time to form the other side of the town..." Uncertain as to whether Reynolds was addressing him, Tremain saluted and rode with orders for the Third corps to "come up."

When Wadsworth's Division reached the Codori Farm, Reynolds pointed him through the fence and sent the column at the double quick across fields on a direct line to the Lutheran Seminary. This column was led by Lysander Cutler's Brigade, followed by Captain James Hall's Second Maine Battery; bringing up the rear was General Solomon Meredith's black-hatted "Iron Brigade," regarded by many as the best brigade in the army. When Cutler's Brigade marched by, one soldier glanced up at the general, and later gave the following description: "General Reynolds sat on his horse on the west side of the highway facing us, and as we marched near the head of the column we had a fair look at his features...the general looked careworn, and we thought, very sad." Very sad indeed. Judging from his earlier remark to Major Tremain, Reynolds was well aware of the desperate, double-sided gamble he had taken. He had committed Buford's cavalry to hold McPherson's Ridge until he could arrive and was wondering whether he could deliver the First Corps and his end of the bargain.

But, John Reynolds and the First Corps did just barely make it, arriving just as Buford's right flank was verging on collapse. Reynolds ordered Cutler up in relief, and the latter sent three regiments dashing across the Chambersburg Pike and the unfinished railroad cut to form a battle line facing west. Cutler's remaining two regiments went into position south of the Pike with their left resting against a wooded lot known as Herbst Woods (mistakenly referred to as McPherson's Woods).

Having placed Cutler's Brigade, Reynolds now summoned Hall's Maine Battery at a trot, and requested to see its commander. Sitting on horseback in the road near McPherson's Barn, the general gave Hall his instructions. "I desire you to damage the artillery to the greatest possible, and keep their fire from our infantry until they are deployed..." At the same time, out of fear that the battery might be vulnerable, Reynolds ordered Wadsworth to provide infantry support on the right. Soon after, a messenger arrived from General Doubleday seeking orders. Reynolds replied that he (and Wadsworth) would handle the Cashtown Road and that Doubleday should deploy the two remaining divisions in defense of the Fairfield Road. Then, at approximately 10:30 a.m., Reynolds glanced into the Herbst Woods beyond the unprotected left flank of the Fourteenth Brooklyn and was stunned by the sight of advancing Confederates.

"FOR GOD'S SAKE FORWARD!"

Somewhat earlier Confederate commander Heth had ordered one of his brigades to cross the stream known as Willoughby Run and push into the woods beyond. As he advanced into them, Brigade Commander James Archer was unaware that his occupation of these woods (Herbst Woods) would severely compromise the entire Federal line. Reynolds knew, however, and having spotted the Rebels, moved quickly to improvise a solution.

Turning about, he spotted elements of Meredith's "Iron Brigade" moving down from the Seminary, and sent two aides to hurry them forward. He then galloped down toward the swale between the two ridges, saw the distinctive black hats of the Second Wisconsin and cried out, "Forward into

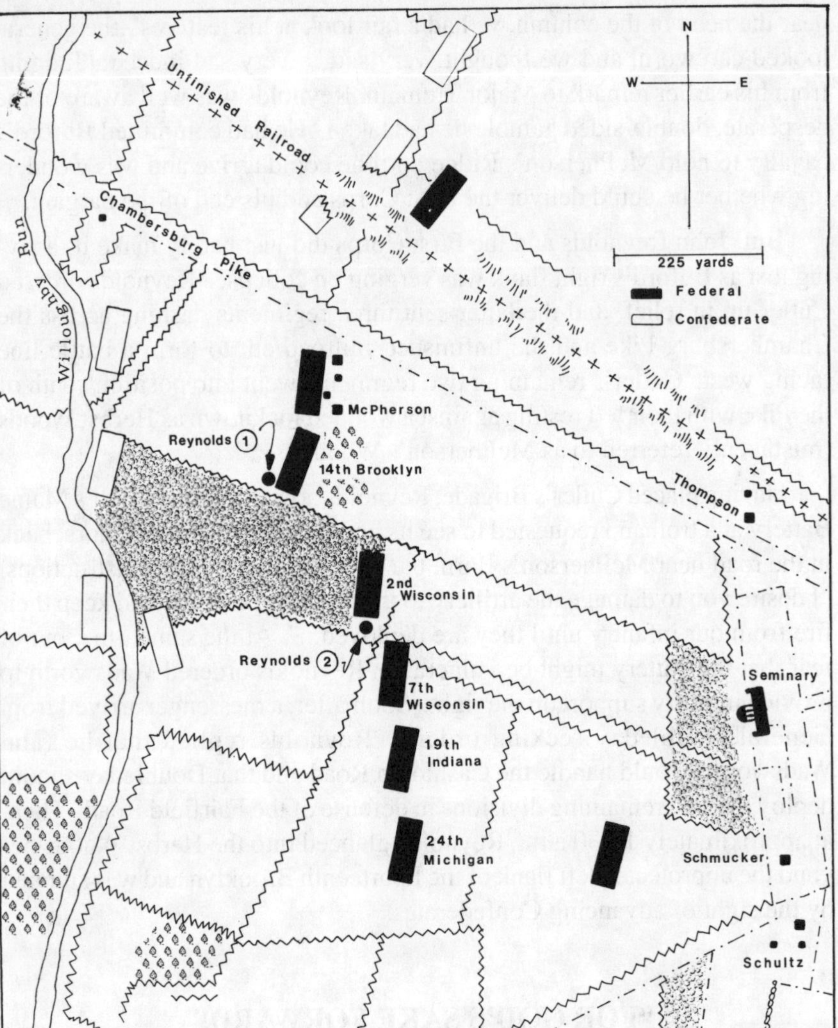

Position 1 indicates the point where General Reynolds first noted the Confederate movement into Herbst Woods.

Position 2 indicates the point where he fell from his horse, shot by a Rebel infantryman.

line at the double quick!..." The Wisconsin men instantly swung into line, trying desperately to load their muskets on the run. As they reached the crest of the ridge they were staggered by a volley from the Rebel line, which inflicted heavy losses while grinding the regiment to a halt. Looking on, Reynolds rode down in among the men to rally them, shouting: "Forward, forward men! Drive those fellows out of that [the woods]. Forward! For God's sake forward!" With Reynolds leading the charge, the Second Wisconsin surged ahead, pushed to the north by tremendous Confederate pressure on their left. Reynolds' orderly, Sergeant Charles Veil, later wrote that "wherever the fight raged the fiercest, there the general was sure to be found, his undaunted courage always inspired the men with more energy and courage."

As the regiment crashed into the woods, riding to the left, Reynolds could see that the Rebels still overlapped his line by a considerable margin. Faced with the danger of being flanked and losing his entire line, he turned in the saddle, looking about for other "Iron Brigade" regiments. Suddenly, his horse bolted forward and the general tumbled to the ground. Three staff members—Captain Edward Baird, Captain Robert Mitchell, and Sergeant Veil—immediately jumped from their horses and went to his aide.

Reynolds was lying on his left side when Veil first reached him. The sergeant rolled him on his back, quickly checked for a wound, but found nothing except a bruise near the left eye. Their immediate concern, however, was not so much his wound as the Rebel firing line, which lay no more than "sixty paces" away. With Veil grabbing him under the arms, and the two captains each taking a leg, they managed to carry him out of the woods. Meanwhile, a number of orderlies rode up, relieving Baird and Mitchell so that they might inform the chain of command.

Veil and two orderlies carried the general back toward the seminary in hopes of finding medical assistance. Crossing the field betwen the two ridges, they heard Reynolds exhale, which led them to believe that he may only have been stunned by a spent minie ball. Veil immediately halted, laid him on the ground and tried to revive him with a drink of water. But, he could not drink, and upon further examination Veil found the wound beneath the general's uniform collar, a small bloodless hole behind the right ear. The men continued on, but at some point during their trek, Dr. J.T. Stillman, a surgeon of the 147th New York, examined the body and announced that the general had died within fifteen minutes of being hit. Quite possibly, the sigh heard by Sergeant Veil was the death gasp of John Reynolds.

At about 11:20 a.m., just at the time that Reynolds was being carried from the field, Captain Weld arrived at army headquarters. Meade had received countless messages that morning, but was waiting most anxiously to hear from Reynolds. As Weld concluded his oral message, Meade exclaimed, "Good! That is just like Reynolds, he will hold on to the bitter end." Then, at approximately 1:00 p.m., Major Riddle rode up with very bad news. Delivering the sad details of Reynolds death, Riddle noted the shock and sorrow on the face of the army commander, now without the services of his chief lieutenant when they were needed most.

But, if he died early in a desperate hour, John Reynolds did not die in vain. The example he set as a loyal subordinate had been crucial during the dark days between the Peninsula and Chancellorsville. The current of trust and confidence between Reynolds and George Meade provided badly needed stability to the army during the late spring of '63. At Gettysburg, he and John Buford ran and *won* perhaps the most dramatic and consequential race in U.S. military history. After his death, his men fought valiantly on where he had placed them, thereby enabling Hancock and Meade to seize and fortify the heights to the south. From this ground, two days later, the battle was won. Truly, when John Reynolds fell, the victorious "architect of the battle had fallen."

EPILOGUE

Reynolds' body was carried to the George House (where he had earlier asked for directions to John Buford) and laid there while staff members searched for a coffin. Two local women later claimed to have assisted the staff in their chores. While watching the body being carried to the rear, Mrs. John Sheads placed her white shawl under his head to comfort him, and upon recovering it found the shawl stained with his blood. Her sister-in-law, Mary Jane Sheads, later stated that the two walked to the George House, and washed the blood from his face while wrapping the body in sheets.

Veil and Captain Joe Rosegarten were unsuccessful in finding a coffin, but did locate a box at a marble cutters. Unfortunately, the length of the box was such that they were forced to knock out one end so that the body could fit. The box was placed in an ambulance at 1:00 p.m. and the sad escort proceded to Union Bridge, Maryland, arriving in late evening. There they procured a coffin in which the corpse was packed with ice. The general was then sent to Baltimore where his brother-in-law made arrangements for embalming and a more suitable coffin. At midnight, July 2, 1863, the body arrived by train in Philadelphia and was taken to 1829 Spruce Street, the home of Mrs. Landis, his sister.

DEAR KATE

While the body lay in the front parlor of the Landis home, a young lady came to the door, and John and Kate Hewitt's secret engagement was finally revealed to his family. During preparation of the body, a chain was discovered around his neck with a heart engraved medallion, and on his finger, where he normally would have worn his West Point class ring, a small ring was found with the inscription "Dear Kate." Inasmuch as John had never mentioned a "Kate" in any of his letters, the family was quite stunned at this discovery and by the arrival of Miss Hewitt at their door.

As she related the tale of her courtship to the Reynolds sisters, they came to regard her as a "superior person." She and John had met, she said, in California in 1860 and fallen in love, and when John had been ordered to West Point, she also had traveled east to attend the Academy of Sacred Heart in Torresdale, Pennsylvania. She was, yes, a Catholic, and she explained that she and John had decided to postpone marriage until after the war. Their agreement had also included Reynolds' permission for her to enter a convent should anything happen to him. This she now intended to do, as the world no longer held her interest.

The initial shock to the Presbyterian Reynolds family was considerable, but after hearing Kate's story, they embraced her as one of their own. Kate Hewitt would become "Sister Hildegardi" after entering the Sisters of Charity Convent in Emmitsburg, Maryland. She remained in touch with the family until 1868, when she disappeared, never to be seen or heard from again.

It is worth noting as well that the Reynolds family never again visited John's patron, former President James Buchanan, at his Wheatland estate in Lancaster. Upon John's death, the relation abruptly ceased. Obviously, the loss of their brother in a war with Buchanan's former associates—"secesh of the first water"—was too much to bear.

John F. Reynolds arrived home in Lancaster, at 11:30 a.m. on July 4, 1863, accompanied by his family and the dedicated members of his staff—Riddle, Mitchell, Rosengarten, Weld, Wilcox, and Veil. The family desired no matrial display for they believed John would not have wanted it, but the streets were filled with people, with flags at half mast and draped with crepe, as the funeral cortege moved slowly to the cemetery. While members of the "Old Reserves" acted as pallbearers, the General was placed beside his mother and father. Captain Weld noted that "a chapter of the Bible was read, and prayer delivered, and then poor General Reynolds disappeared from us for some time to come." At the moment of interment, Major Riddle fell to the ground and wept.

A month after the battle the Reynolds family received a request from the "Old First Brigade" of the Reserve Division asking that one of their members be allowed to travel to Philadelphia to make a presentation. These men had decided after the Battle of Mechanicsville (June 1862) to present the general with a sword, belt, and sash "in a testimony of their love and admiration." The sword was made of the finest Damascus steel, and the scabbard was of pure gold. The grip was adorned with black onyx with his initials—J.F.R.—set in diamonds; on the reverse was a scroll with the Latin inscription "Vincer Amor Patriae" (Love of Country Conquers). The men had carried the sword in a company wagon during the Gettysburg campaign, in hopes of making the presentation themselves, but to their great sorrow, never had a chance.

In September 1863 the Reynolds family received another request, this one from the entire First Corps, asking permission to raise money for a monument to be erected "as a small tribute to his memory...which would please the officers and men of the old Corps." Of the many tributes Reynolds received, those of the Pennsylvania Reserves and the First Corps would have undoubtedly meant the most.

Top—Catherine Mary Hewitt as "Sister Hildegardi."
Picture taken in Philadelphia, December 1863, four months after Reynolds' death at Gettysburg.
(Courtesy Franklin and Marshall College)

Bottom—Catherine Mary Hewitt, General Reynolds' fianceé and secret love, circa 1860–1862. *(Courtesy Franklin and Marshall College)*

The man whom Abraham Lincoln would call "our gallant and brave friend" had placed the good of the army and the cause of Union above personal ambition and made the ultimate sacrifice at Gettysburg. That he did so came as no surprise to those who loved him, and even Kate Hewitt accepted his priorities. In her heart, she had given him first "to God, then to his country, and then to herself." About her own sacrifice there lingers a haunting sadness.

Afterword
REYNOLDS OF GETTYSBURG

Great events are typically made up of a series of small incidents. This was certainly true of the titanic three days at Gettysburg in 1863. Some of these smaller incidents are significant in and of themselves in that they had critical impact on the course and outcome of the great event. The actions of Maj. Gen. John F. Reynolds on the first day of the battle were such significant and decisive incidents. It is appropriate to emphasize Reynolds' involvement, his last and finest hour. One may first identify him, to see him as a general officer.

In several ways, Reynolds was typical of the ranking generals of the Army of the Potomac. Thus he was politically conservative, a pre-war Democrat antagonistic to abolition. On the other hand, he was intensely committed to the Union, a patriot in a very real sense and angry about secession. His military philosophy was similarly conservative. Like McClellan, he believed that the war should have been in the hands of the military, free and clear of the political objectives and necessities of the government and uninhibited by civilian control. He perceived a nonexistent line between politics and war, and between the government and its military forces. Under this extra-constitutional view, the Washington administration should not have had the jurisdiction or the power to decide and direct the military establishment. Reynolds' inability to structure army command in this way caused him to reject the offer of command of the Army of the Potomac.

His concept of warfare was also traditional. He was initially skeptical of volunteer soldiers, was a strict disciplinarian, and believed in the protection of the private property of the enemy. Despite these characteristics, Reynolds was highly popular with his Washington superiors and his military peers and those he commanded, both officers and enlisted men. Unlike other major military figures of the Eastern theater, he was discreet with his politics and was not an intriguer. The commands of Burnside and Hooker had been marked by political intrigue and jockeying. Reynolds and Meade, who was junior to Reynolds, had long been friendly rivals. They cooperated on Meade's appointment to command and brought on a needed period of stability to the army.

Douglas Southall Freeman has written that Lee's "army...had been wrecked at Gettysburg." Without belaboring the classic issue of the decisiveness of that battle in terms of the war, it is surely fair to say that the Confederate defeat was highly damaging. It forever limited Lee's capacity to maneuver and thus predicted the ultimate siege which led to his surrender. There has been much careless writing about Gettysburg's first day. Confederate apologists sometimes speak of a Confederate victory on the first day, as if July 1 represented a battle in and of itself without reference to the succeeding two days and as if unmindful of what the stakes were on July 1. Other writers, referring to the Federals, use such words as "swept from the field," "collapsed," and "fled" to describe the action of the Eleventh and First Corps. The Federals were indeed defeated on the first day but their dogged and desperate fighting had permitted Federal possession of the key ground and had purchased the time for the Army of the Potomac to gather on that ground. Lee reported that the four Confederate divisions engaged on the first day were "weakened and exhausted by a long and bloody struggle," which surely contradicts the image of Federals that were "swept away."

The truth is that at stake on the first day of Gettysburg were two factors critical to the battle's outcome, *field position* and *time.* The key ground was the high ground south of the town: Cemetery Hill, Culp's Hill, Cemetery Ridge and the Round Tops. Possession of these heights—Porter Alexander called them "a position unique among all the battlefields of the war"—provided a significant Federal advantage. And time was essential so that the several missing corps of the Army of the Potomac could gather to defend this ground. These factors were what the first day of the battle was all about. The Federals held the ground and acquired the time. John F. Reynolds was the principal agent of these accomplishments.

Crediting Reynolds on the first day does not mitigate the contribution of Brig. Gen. John Buford. Screening the advance of the army's left wing, Buford initially established a cavalry line on July 1, west and north of Gettysburg as the divisions of Heth, Pender, Rodes and Early moved toward town. The horsemen's skillful and tenacious defense afforded Reynolds his opportunity. Ordered by Meade to advance his First Corps to Gettysburg early on July 1, with the Eleventh Corps in support, it was Reynolds' decision to fight at McPherson's Ridge, and his bringing up the Eleventh Corps, that created the defense in depth of the high ground south of the town. This defense set up the ultimate battle site on that high ground.

It is only fair to note that Reynolds' decision was especially timely in the light of Meade's obvious uncertainty. Meade's order that sent the first corps to Gettysburg said that he would "assume position for offensive or defensive, as occasion requires, or rest to the troops." Uncertainty marked another of Meade's communications to Reynolds on July 1: "The commanding general cannot decide whether it is his best policy to move to attack until he learns something more definite of the point at which the enemy is concentrating...Meanwhile, he would like to have your views upon the subject." This communication proceeded to discuss whether or not Gettysburg was the appropriate place for a Federal concentration and again solicited Reynolds' "suggestions." It is generally believed that Reynolds did not receive this latter communication, or the more or less simultaneous Pipe Creek Circular, but his actions plainly established his views of the proper role and place for the Army of the Potomac.

Significantly, after Reynolds' death a series of commanders on the field ratified Reynolds' decision. Doubleday, Howard, and finally Hancock clung to McPherson's and Seminary Ridges until the Federals were withdrawn, and the Federal Corps then assembled on the "position unique" from which Lee was heavily defeated. Lost Cause writers and Lee apologists have tried to diminish the Federal accomplishments on the first day by reiterating the "Ewell card": only Ewell's wrong-headed failure to attack Cemetery Hill permitted the Federals to hold the advantageous field position. These commentators forget that Lee was on the field and did not order such an attack. He also justified Ewell in his official report.

John F. Reynolds' death at Gettysburg has guaranteed his status as a romantic hero of the war. It is well to remember that this supreme contribution was matched by his tactical judgement.

Alan T. Nolan
Indianapolis, IN

EDITORS NOTE: Alan T. Nolan's writings include *The Iron Brigade* and *Lee Considered: General Robert E. Lee and Civil War History*. He has also published in the major Civil War and historical journals and resides in Indianapolis. He is a Fellow of the Company of Military Historians and a member of the Indianapolis Civil War Round Table.

READERS NOTE: The endnotes of this work have been placed on file for viewing purposes at the Gettysburg National Military Park Library. Readers may obtain a set of endnotes by sending $2.00 to the Farnsworth House Book Shop, 401 Baltimore St., Gettysburg, PA, 17325.

SELECT BIBLIOGRAPHY

Aimone, Alan & Barbara. "Much to Sadden and Little to Cheer: The Civil War Years at West Point." *Blue and Gray Magazine*. Issue No. 2 1991.

Bachelder, John. *Gettysburg in Their Own Words*. Volume 1. January 5, 1863 to July 27, 1880. Dayton, Ohio: Morningside House, Inc. 1994.

Cleaves, Freeman. *Meade of Gettysburg*. Oklahoma: Norman and London. University of Oklahoma Press, 1960.

Coddington, Edwin B. *The Gettysburg Campaign.* New York: Charles Scribner's Sons, 1968.

Doubleday, Abner. *Chancellorsville and Gettysburg*. New York: DaCapo Press, 1994.

Hassler Jr., Warren W. *Crisis at the Crossroads*. Tuscaloosa, Alabama: University of Alabama Press, 1970.

Hennessy, John J. *Return to Bull Run*. New York: Simon and Schuster Co., 1993.

Henry, Robert Selph. *The Story of the Mexican War*. New York: Da Capo Press, 1950.

Lewis, Lloyd. *Captain Sam Grant 1822-1861*. Volume 1. Boston: Little, Brown and Co., 1950.

Maloney, Mary. "General Reynolds and Dear Kate." *American Heritage Magazine.* Volume XV, No. 1.

Martin, David G. *Gettysburg July 1*. Conshohocken, Pennsylvania: Combined Books, 1995.

Morrison Jr., James L. *The Best School in the World, West Point, the Pre-Civil War Years 1833-1866*. Kent, Ohio: Kent State University Press, 1962.

Pfanz, Harry W. *Gettysburg: Culp's Hill and Cemetery Hill*. Chapel Hill and London: University of North Carolina Press, 1993.

Sears, Stephen W. *George B. McClellan, The Young Napoleon*. New York: Ticknor and Fields, 1968.

Scott, Colonel John Fulton Reynolds. "John Fulton Reynolds," Lancaster County Historical Society Papers. Volume LII. No. 2, 1948.

Shue, Richard S. *Morning at Willoughby Run, July 1, 1863*. Gettysburg, Pennsylvania: Thomas Publications, 1995.

Smith, Major General William Farrar. "Franklin's Left Grand Division" *Battles and Leaders of the Civil War.* Retreat from Gettysburg. New York: Castle Books, 1956.

Steiner, Paul E. M.D., PH.D. *Medical-Military Portraits of Union and Confederate Generals,* Philadelphia: Whitemore Publishing Co., 1968.

Sypher, J.R. Esq. *History of the Pennsylvania Reserve Corps,* Pennsylvania: Elias Barr and Co., 1865.

United States War Department. *The War of the Rebellion: A Compilation of the Official Records of the Union and Confederate Armies.* Washington, D.C.: Government Printing Office, 1880-1901. Volume 27, Parts 1, 2, and 3.

Viola, Herman J. *The Memoirs of Charles Henry Veil, The History of the American West.* New York: Orion Books, 1993.

Weld, Stephen Minot. *War Diary and Letters,* Boston: Massachusetts Historical Society, 1979.

Woodward, Evan Morrison. *Our Campaigns, The Second Regiment Pennsylvania Volunteers 1861-1864.* Edited by Stanley W. Zamonski. Pennsylvania: Burd Street Press, 1995.

Reynolds Family Papers (MS6), Archives and Special Collections Department, Franklin and Marshall College, Lancaster, PA.

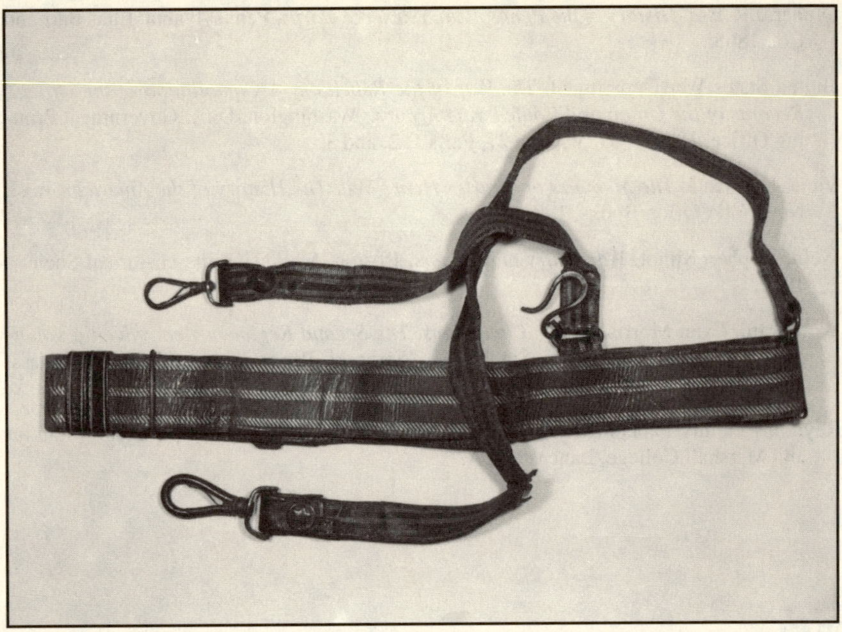

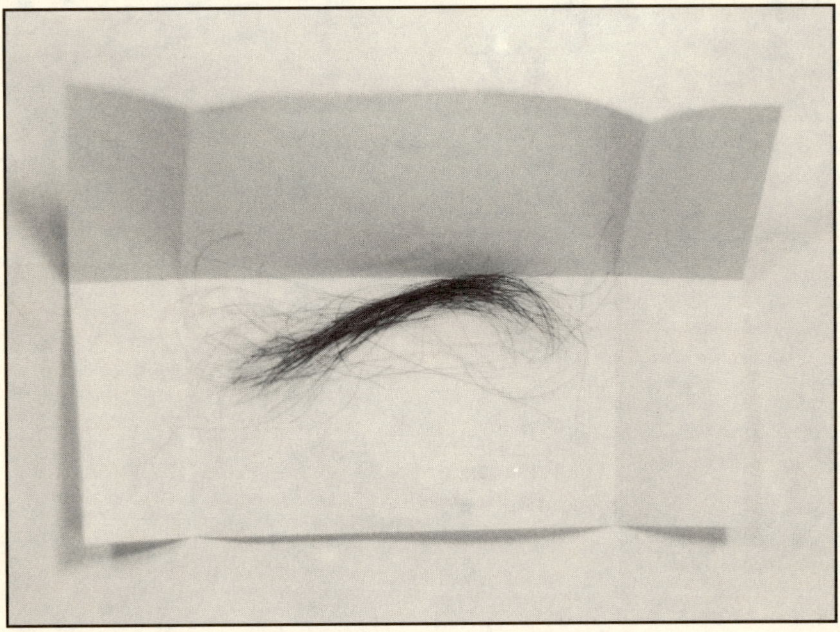

Top—General Reynolds' sword belt.
(Courtesy Franklin and Marshall College)

Bottom—A lock of John Reynolds' hair.
(Courtesy Franklin and Marshall College)

Author Michael A. Riley is a native of Lancaster, Pennsylvania and is a member of Co. E., Thirtieth Pennsylvania (First PA Reserves), following in his great-grandfather John B. Riley's footsteps. He has been researching and lecturing on the life of John F. Reynolds for the past eight years. A commercial roofing salesman by trade, he was hired in the summer of 1992 to act as a consultant and double to actor John Rothman for the motion picture *Gettysburg*. He is now actively working on the Reynolds' Family Papers, transcribing and editing for future publication.

FARNSWORTH HOUSE PUBLICATIONS

"TRUST IN GOD AND FEAR NOTHIN": GEN. LEWIS A. ARMISTEAD, CSA, by Wayne E. Motts, w/afterword by Lewis B. Armistead. Farnsworth House Civil War Commander Series #1.

"THE DEVIL'S TO PAY!": GEN. JOHN BUFORD, USA, by Michael Phipps & John S. Peterson, w/afterword by Senator Tom Buford. Farnsworth House Civil War Commander Series #2.

"FAITHFULLY AND FOREVER YOUR SOLDIER": GEN. GEORGE E. PICKETT, CSA, by Richard F. Selcer, w/afterword by George E. Pickett. Farnsworth House Civil War Commander Series #3.

"FOR GOD'S SAKE, FORWARD!": GEN. JOHN F. REYNOLDS, USA, by Michael A. Riley, w/afterword by Alan T. Nolan. Farnsworth House Civil War Commander Series #4.

TRAVELLER & COMPANY: THE HORSES OF GETTYSBURG, by Blake A. Magner, w/forword by Mark Myers.

THE BATTLE OF GETTYSBURG, by Major General George Gordon Meade. (Self contained extract from Gen. Mead's Life & Letters, edited by his son.)